Study Skills and Dyslexia in the Secondary School

Study Skills and Dyslexia in the Secondary School

A practical approach

MARION GRIFFITHS

David Fulton Publishers
London

For Peter, Victoria and James

David Fulton Publishers Ltd
414 Chiswick High Road, London W4 5TF

www.fultonpublishers.co.uk

First published in Great Britain by David Fulton Publishers 2002
Reprinted 2003
10 9 8 7 6 5 4 3 2

Note: The right of Marion Griffiths to be identified as the author of this work has been asserted by her in accordance with the Copyright, Designs and Patents Act 1988.

Copyright © Marion Griffiths 2002

British Library Cataloguing in Publication Data
A catalogue record for this book is available from the British Library.

ISBN 1–85346–790–1

Typeset by FiSH Books, London
Printed and bound in Great Britain by Ashford Colour Press Limited, Gosport, Hants

Contents

Acknowledgements

I would like to thank all the staff at David Fulton Publishers for giving me the opportunity to write this book. I am also grateful for all the support I have received from everyone at David Fulton Publishers. I am indebted to Jude Bowen, Kirsty Bevan, Dr Stephen Bigger, Roz Hanna, Ann Caborn, Matt Jones, Paul Hooker, Colin Caborn, Priscilla Sharland, Alan Worth, Georgina Allen and Rachael Robertson for offering their specific expertise. I am grateful to the many schools who responded to the Study Skills Schools' Survey. As always, I have appreciated the inspiration and continuous support of my family.

Introduction

Why write a book about study skills for students with dyslexia between the ages of 11–18?

The reason for writing this book is to relieve students of the burden of examinations and schoolwork. Study support programmes benefit *all* students, often leading to higher grades in GCSEs (MacBeath *et al.* 2001). Furthermore, the impact of recent curriculum changes particularly those at post-16 has placed increased pressure upon schools to seek new teaching approaches which allow students to reach their full potential. Essentially, study skills are a stepping stone to academic achievements for *all* students, however, the difference for dyslexic learners, is that they will *rely* upon specific strategies to acquire similar successes. Ultimately, effective study skills can provide a gateway to independent lifelong learning and a wider choice of career opportunities.

How is this book to be used?

Based upon theory, this practical and accessible book is aimed at specialist and non-specialist practitioners seeking to improve study skills. It is essential that Special Educational Needs Coordinators (SENCOs) are kept fully informed throughout the process of identification, assessment and delivery of teaching of secondary students with dyslexia. There are checklists and worksheets for SENCOs, subject teachers, Learning Support Assistants, student teachers, Newly Qualified Teachers, parents and secondary learners. It has been recognised that dyslexics have specific individual educational requirements which accounts for adopting a detailed, structured holistic approach to assessment and teaching. It is possible to read the book in the order in which it is presented; however, as this is a practical handbook, each chapter may be read or referred to in *any* order, making use of the cross-references where necessary. For this reason, a wide range and choice of resources and addresses have been listed. As professionals, we must continue to recognise, nurture, cherish and celebrate the valuable contribution dyslexic learners can make as worthwhile citizens.

What is meant by the term study skills?

The term study skills is used here to refer to: organisational skills, note-taking skills, writing, reading, memory, revision and examination techniques. Before this book was written, 50 secondary schools were contacted to obtain a current insight about key practices associated with dyslexic learners and study skills. The book contains qualitative research which gives an additional practical insight to study skills and dyslexia in the secondary school.

Schools' Survey

What do you understand by the term study skills?

Schools maintained that study skills involved: note-taking, library research, reading, organisational skills, retaining and understanding information, revision and examination skills.

PART 1

Assessment and secondary students with dyslexia

1 Dyslexia and assessment

This chapter offers guidance to secondary personnel in approaching the initial assessment of students considered to be dyslexic. There is a brief history of dyslexia, and definitions of dyslexia are examined from a theoretical perspective. There is a checklist to determine visual, auditory and speech strengths and limitations of students. In addition there is a checklist for parents/guardians who can assist in assessing and supporting the student and a self-assessment worksheet for the student to complete. The legal requirements of the Revised Code of Practice (DfES 2002) and the American Individuals with Disabilities Education Act (IDEA 1997) are discussed. The chapter concludes with a list of suggestions for motivating secondary students' learning.

Introduction

Formal and informal assessment approaches are integrated as part of the national educational system and teachers' daily routine for raising standards in effective learning for all secondary students, including those with dyslexia. Standardised assessment tests can be administered to discover if students require special provision and to highlight students' individual strengths and limitations. Through enlisting academic and non-academic support throughout students' education it is envisaged that any perceived limitations will be short-lived. Theory has been used to underpin dyslexia and assessment. Central to this assessment process is the SENCO who must be kept fully informed at all times. The SENCO is a specialist teacher who takes an active role in ensuring that progress is made by students with special educational needs, including those with dyslexia. Among the many duties undertaken by the SENCO are advising school staff and parents and liaising with external experts.

Prior to assessing a student for dyslexia a secondary teacher should consider the answers to a checklist of questions. The objective of this checklist is to provide direction to the student assessment.

3

Checklist of questions teacher should ask prior to student assessment

1. What is the purpose of assessment? What do you need to discover about the student that you do not already know?
2. What resources are necessary for assessment?
3. How and where is the assessment going to take place?
4. Do students understand why they are being assessed?
5. What is the best way to give feedback to students and how is it going to benefit them? What are the implications of the student assessment for the curriculum? Do students agree or disagree with their assessment?
6. What is the appropriate format for circulating information from the student assessment to other interested parties?
7. What actions do students need to take following assessment?

A brief history of dyslexia

In 1846 Pringle Morgan taught a 14-year-old boy named Percy who had difficulty spelling words with more than one syllable. He wrote his name as 'Precy'. His teacher declared that 'he would be the smartest lad in the school if the instruction were entirely oral' (Morgan 1896). This identification has similarities with the former Code of Practice (DFE 1994) which claims that pupils may have good oral skills yet may experience difficulty with spelling. In 1861, Broca claimed that the inability to use language properly could be due to aphasia or damage to the brain (Miles and Miles 1990). Head (1926) echoed the same idea years later by suggesting that thoughts and speech could be affected by aphasia.

Kussmaul (1878) was the first person to identify 'word blindness' and 'word deafness'. This theme was later developed in 1900 by James Hinshelwood, a Glaswegian eye surgeon, who explained his term of 'congenital word blindness' as:

> a congenital defect occurring in children with otherwise normal and undamaged brains characterised by a difficulty in learning to read so great that it is manifestly due to a pathological condition, and where the attempt to teach the child by ordinary methods have completely failed.
>
> (Hinshelwood 1917, p. 19)

Hinshelwood concluded that dyslexia could be hereditary and more frequent in boys than girls.

In 1937 Samuel Orton, an American neurologist considered that dyslexia was 'strephosymbolia' (twisting of symbols) rather than 'word blindness' when reading or spelling words. That is to say, words could be distorted. Studies on the subject of eye movements by Zangwill and Blakemore (1972) concluded that poor readers sometimes display erratic eye movements.

Dyslexia was first mentioned in the Chronically Sick and Disabled Persons Act in 1970, section 27 (DES 1970). Two years later this was followed by the

Tizard Report (1972), which claimed that children with dyslexia had weaknesses with reading, writing, spelling and number. The emphasis of dyslexia was changed from reading to language difficulties in the Bullock Report (1975). From 1978 onwards it was recognised that children with special educational needs including those with dyslexia would require further consideration and special provision. The Warnock Report (1978), and the 1981 Education Act (DES 1981) gave children with dyslexia access to the main curriculum and it became feasible for a pupil with specific learning difficulties to have his or her special educational needs protected by the issuing of a 'statement of special educational needs' by the Local Educational Authority (LEA).

Definitions of dyslexia and assessment of secondary students

Differing definitions of dyslexia by acclaimed experts offer an insight to professionals to identify, assess and monitor pupils' progress. Definitions of dyslexia provide a platform to compare and contrast with classroom practice. Frequently, dyslexia has been portrayed in literature as a 'deficit model' or as a negative condition. Current thinking has changed slightly to reflect a positive paradigm shift (West 1997). Students with dyslexia may have identified abilities which coexist alongside identified disabilities.

Schools in England and Wales currently need to be aware of the changes being made to the Revised Code of Practice which comes into effect in January 2002. Moving from the former Code's (DFE 1994) precise definition of dyslexia the consultation document for the new Revised Code's (DfEE 2001) global definition recognises that dyslexics may have abilities and limitations in two precise areas, namely, 'communication and interaction' and 'cognition and learning'. Practitioners may also consider that sometimes dyslexics fall into the two other special educational needs (SEN) categories of – 'behaviour, emotional and social development' and 'sensory and or physical needs'.

English legislation is echoed in the American Individuals With Disabilities Education Act (IDEA 1997) which initially defines dyslexia generally before being termed as a 'condition':

(A) In general – The term 'specific learning disability' means a disorder in one or more of the basic psychological processes involved in understanding or in using language, spoken or written, which disorder may manifest itself in imperfect ability to listen, think, speak, read, write, spell or do mathematical calculations.

(B) Disorders included – Such terms includes conditions as perceptual disabilities, brain injury, minimal brain dysfunction, dyslexia, and developmental aphasia. (p. 13)

Johnson and Mykelebust (1967) suggest visual dyslexics may have difficulty noticing internal detail and that their rate of perception may be slow.

Stein (1991) has demonstrated through research that 'visual impairments cause specific kinds of reading error'. It could mean that learners with dyslexia may have difficulty grasping abstract concepts in the curriculum if they have poor perceptual skills. Where possible informed professionals should refer to concrete examples in their teaching. During a diagnostic assessment it may mean that students could be slow at pointing to an object in a visual discrimination exercise. Students affected with poor visual discrimination may also have 'reversal tendencies in both reading and writing', for example 'dig' may be read for 'big' (Miles 1991). Sometimes the use of coloured filters or overlays placed over texts during reading can lead to improved results. It is advisable to visit a good optician for further information on the subject.

Many experts consider that biological causes are at the root of dyslexia. Duane (1991) and Stein (1991) suggest that dyslexia may be a misfunction of the brain which could coexist alongside other disorders such as Attention Deficit Hyperactivity Disorder (ADHD). However, Stein argues that phonological and visuospatial impairments may arise in dyslexics because of the disordered development of the right hemisphere in the brain. Writing from a medical viewpoint Carter (1996) suggests that dyslexia is caused by a faulty connection between two areas of the brain. DeFries (1991) observes that dyslexia often tends to run in families and is of the opinion that it has neurological and genetic origins, while Paulesu *et al.* (1996) report that members of the same family may be affected differently by the condition. It is widely recognised that failure to read and write can be caused by a speech processing difficulty.

Auditory dyslexics may find it difficult to discriminate short vowel sounds or recognise rhymes (Miles 1996). Students with this difficulty may find it hard to break down words into syllables; they cannot remember letter sounds, they cannot say the word even knowing the meaning and are unable to remember the rhythmic pattern. They perform poorly in tasks involving auditory memory sequence and discrimination. Taken to the extreme, it could mean that poor hearing results in poor phonological ability and spelling. Examining students' educational history should offer an insight into where visual and auditory strengths and limitations lie.

Vellutino (1987) claims that dyslexia refers to the extraordinary difficulty experienced by otherwise normal children in learning to identify printed words. He believes the root of dyslexia lies in the visual spatial system. In the classroom context, staff need to observe if vision is limiting students' progress. Checking students' vision includes the following: whether learners rub their eyes, hold books too close to their eyes, squint when looking at the blackboard/whiteboard or bump into objects. Opticians and optometrists may need to be consulted for further visual advice.

West (1997) points out that some neurologists use the term dyslexia in its more global and literal sense by saying that 'dys' refers to 'difficulty' and 'lexia' refers to 'words', simply difficulty with words. Usage of this term includes difficulty with decoding written symbols into spoken sounds or verbal meaning, and includes other related problems, such as recalling names, difficulty finding the right words or hesitant speech. Stanovich (1991) maintains that dyslexics have an 'unexpected' disability where reading is concerned which is not predicted by their intelligence or sociocultural opportunities.

The following teacher's observational checklist is designed to pinpoint initial visual, auditory or speech factors which could affect students' learning. If the student displays visual, auditory or speech difficulties medical advice should be sought. An Individual Education Plan (IEP) may be used to address identified visual, auditory or speech limitations in secondary students.

Checklist of visual, auditory and speech observations

1. Does the student have a history of eye problems?
2. Should the student wear glasses for your lessons?
3. Does the student wear glasses or contact lenses all the time?
4. Does the student hold textbooks very close to his/her eyes?
5. Does the student bump into furniture, people or other objects?
6. Can written errors and/or poor presentation be attributed to poor eyesight?
7. Does the student rub his/her eyes?
8. Does the student misread words?
9. Eyes are a good indicator of health, does the student have a history of health problems outside the norm?
10. Does the student have a history of hearing problems?
11. Does the student ask for words to be repeated?
12. Does the student lean forward to hear what is being said?
13. Does the student have difficulty following oral instructions in class?
14. Does the student have a history of speech delay?
15. Does the student mispronounce words?
16 Does the student stutter or stammer?
17. Can the secondary student give a logical oral account of what he/she did in the holidays, a book which has been read, or a film which has been seen?

Although a complex task, assessment of a secondary learner's cognitive ability is useful as there 'are hundreds of skills to be considered' (West 1997). Hassett defines cognitive ability as being a 'human behaviour that emphasises the active internal nature of higher mental processes involved in such areas as attention, memory, perception, language, imagery, and reasoning' (1984, p. 601). One of the common indicators of bright dyslexics is that there is a distinctive peak and valley pattern in intelligence tests and other measures of ability (West 1997).

The following observational checklist is intended to provide initial indicators of secondary students' cognitive ability from which professionals can deliver teaching to correspond to students' educational requirements.

Checklist of observations to provide initial indicators of cognitive skills

1. Does the student react appropriately in the school environment?
2. Which activities sustain the student's interest?

3. Does the student think more in pictures than in words? Does the student find it easier to draw or illustrate what he/she means rather than explain it orally or in writing?
4. Does the student demonstrate a natural ability towards any of the curriculum subjects?
5. In what way could the student use all his/her senses in his/her academic subjects throughout the curriculum?
6. In what way does the student express his/her imagination throughout the curriculum?
7. Does the student have good concentration and attention span during lessons?
8. What strategies does the student use for remembering?
9. Can the student remember what he/she covered from the last lesson?
10. Can the student understand and perceive abstract concepts in all his/ her curriculum subjects?

Legislative requirements of the Revised Code of Practice (DfES 2002) and the American Individuals with Disabilities Education Act (IDEA 1997)

There are many parallels between special educational provision in England and Wales and the USA and they are as follows:

1. SEN legislation in England and Wales and the USA has undergone recent changes. The Code of Practice and SEN regulations have been revised and come into effect together with the SEN Disability Bill by the DfES in England and Wales in 2002. During 1997 the Individuals with Disabilities Education Act (IDEA) was amended in the USA.
2. Both the Revised Code of Practice and the IDEA (1997) are divided into sections.
3. Both the Revised Code of Practice and the IDEA (1997) use Individual Education Plans (UK) or Programs (USA) to develop, monitor and review student progress.
4. Both documents seek to promote high expectations of those students with special educational needs including those with dyslexia in mainstream schools.
5. Both documents stress the importance of developing effective partnerships with parents.

Schools' Survey

Schools were sent questionnaires on the subject of dyslexia and study skills before the Revised Code of Practice had been published.

Do you consider The Code of Practice (DFE 1994) an effective and practical document for assessing the study skills of secondary students with dyslexia?

There was an emphatic 'No' from all respondents. Additional comments were as follows:

- *'significant that the Revised Code omits reference to severe learning difficulties (SLDs) (including dyslexia) . . . not a "working" document';*
- *'far too primary based';* and
- *'I wouldn't suggest this is the aim/function of the Code of Practice, it has more to do with standardising/enabling special needs provision and priorities.'*

The Revised Code of Practice comes into effect in January 2002. Associated with the Revised Code is the SEN Disability Bill. This document was given Royal assent in May 2001 and emphasises the educational rights of disabled children to be treated equally in mainstream schools. The consultation document for the Revised Code of Practice (DfEE 2001) offers shorter, clearer guidance on the role of responsibilities of LEAs and schools. There are sections devoted to identification, assessment and provision in EarlyYears, the Primary Phase and the Secondary Sector. Greater prominence in the revised document is given to the rights of parents, pupil participation and practical support in the classroom.

Table 1.1 outlines how the statutory five-staged model of procedures for the assessment of special educational needs in the former Code of Practice (DFE 1994) has been reduced to three in the Revised Code (DfES 2002).

Table 1.1 Comparison of procedures for SEN assessment between the Revised (DfES 2002) and former Code of Practice (DFE 1994)

Revised Code (DfES 2002)	Former Code (DFE 1994, p. 3)
School Action	*Stage 1:* class or subject teachers identify or register a child's special educational needs and, consulting the school's SENCO take initial action
	Stage 2: the school's SENCO takes lead responsibility for gathering information and for coordinating the child's special educational provision, working with the child's teachers
School Action Plus	*Stage 3:* teachers and the SENCO are supported by specialists from outside the school
Statement	*Stage 4:* the LEA consider the need for a statutory assessment and, if appropriate, make a multi-disciplinary assessment
	Stage 5: the LEA consider the need for a statement of special educational needs and, if appropriate make a statement and arrange, and review provision

The Revised Code (DfES 2002) is divided into three sections which correspond with recognised age group divisions in the UK educational system: Identification, Assessment and Provision in Early Education Settings; Identification, Assessment and Provision in the Primary Phase and Identification, Assessment and Provision in the Secondary Sector. Whereas, the IDEA (1997) is divided into four parts:

Part A – 'General Provisions' explains the purpose and how special education law works;

Part B – 'Assistance for Education of all Children with Disabilities' explains funding, evaluation, eligibility, individualised education programs, educational placements and other services relating to administration;

Part C – 'Infants and Toddlers with Disabilities' explains services available to this group and

Part D – 'National Activities to Improve Education of Children with Disabilities' recognises that a pro-active approach is needed to improve the services of special education, for example, through retraining of specialist personnel and educational research.

It can be argued, that through the Revised Code's staged approach, good communication is necessary among educational professionals for students to derive benefit. The Revised Code emphasises that children with special educational needs, including those with dyslexia, must have access to a broad education including the National Curriculum. At the heart of the Revised Code is the underlying theme of 'concern' which is used to identify and assess students. At School Action, the class or subject teachers identify or register a child's special educational needs, and by consulting the school's Special Educational Needs Coordinator (SENCO), take initial action. It is recognised at this initial gathering of information that it is a process of bringing together everything which is currently known about the child to enable future planning (Russell 1994). Then the school's SENCO takes responsibility for gathering information and for coordinating the child's educational provision while working with the student's teachers and any curriculum specialists. Normally, SENCOs draw up an Individual Education Plan (IEP).

The IEP underpins the curriculum which the student is already following; it makes use of programmes, activities, materials and assessment techniques easily available to the student's teachers and sets clear teaching and learning targets with monitoring arrangements. It may clarify any additional pastoral or medical requirements. IEPs are required to be reviewed frequently. This allows the assessment of progress while providing an opportunity to seek further advice, update information and to develop the IEP further. Parents and pupils are encouraged to be part of this regular review system of improvement by expressing their views.

At School Action Plus teachers and the SENCO are supported by specialists from outside the school. The LEA may consider the need for a statutory assessment and make a multi-disciplinary assessment. The third stage of the Revised Code is when the LEA may consider the need for a statement of special educational needs and where appropriate make a statement. At this stage reviewing provision may take place. It is the professional's responsibility to be aware of the school's special educational needs policy.

Technically the Revised Code of Practice and the National Curriculum apply to the secondary school, nevertheless, it can be useful for secondary staff to have an awareness of *The National Literacy Strategy* (DfEE 1998). Grammar, punctuation and themes outlined in this document may need to be revisited in IEPs at secondary level. The professional's skill lies in interpreting these mandatory documents and applying them in a beneficial way for scholars.

Assessment checklists for secondary students

The following checklists are a preliminary attempt to discover the student's natural strengths and limitations while simultaneously obtaining a picture of his/her performance in the curriculum. As a consequence of completing these initial checklists professionals will determine which teaching strategies and resources can be selected to develop specific skills in secondary students.

Checklist for teachers' assessment of students' performance in the curriculum

1. What aspects of reading does the student find easy?
2. Which aspects of reading does the student find difficult?
3. How does the student's reading compare with his/her peers?
4. What aspects of writing does the student find easy?
5. Which aspects of the student's written work need to be addressed?
6. How does the student's written work compare with his/her peers?
7. What are the student's spelling strengths?
8. Which aspects of the student's spelling need to be addressed?
9. How does the student's spelling compare to those of his/her peers?
10. What are the student's mathematical strengths?
11. Which aspects of the student's mathematical skills need addressing?
12. How does the student's mathematical ability compare to that of his/her peers?
13. What observations can be made about the student's behaviour towards teachers, peers and towards other people's property?
14. Does the student display any preferences to teaching and learning where the following are concerned:
    (a) visual?
    (b) auditory?
    (c) speech?
    (d) memory?
    (e) organisation?
15. When and under which circumstances does the student produce poor quality work?
16. What are the student's academic and non-academic strengths and limitations?

Secondary student's self-assessment of educational profile

Student involvement in educational issues may lead to positive outcomes throughout the curriculum. Student participation in learning often leads to increased motivation which results in academic progress being made.

The secondary student's self-assessment of educational profile worksheet can be useful to subject teachers in gathering information about students for whom there may be concerns. The aim of the worksheet is to enlighten the professional at key points throughout the learner's education. It is always valuable to have a record of the student's perception of himself/herself to compare and contrast with the professional's. The worksheet could be administered in the following ways: either as a written or oral exercise, as a class exercise or with students in a one-to-one situation.

Parents/guardians' assessment of their son or daughter

Parents/guardians can supply school staff with information which can be of great assistance in developing the student's educational needs. They can be assured that information of a sensitive and confidential nature which could be of use will be treated in a professional manner. Information from the parents/guardians' assessment checklist would be useful to staff when students start their secondary education. Schools are only too happy to foster effective home–school partnerships and there will be many opportunities for parents to impart the information from this checklist during their son or daughter's schooling – such as open days and parents' evenings. Clearly, information will change as the student progresses through their education.

Checklist for parents/guardians' assessment of their son or daughter

Name of son/daughter: ....

1. Is there anything in your son or daughter's medical records that the school needs to be informed about?
2. Does the school need to be informed about any of the changes in home circumstances?
3. Does you son/daughter wear glasses?
4. Does your son or daughter have good hearing?
5. Has your son or daughter any special interests or hobbies?
6. What books or magazines does your son/daughter read?
7. What is your son/daughter's attitude towards school?
8. What is your son/daughter's attitude towards homework?
9. How does your son/daughter treat you?
10. How does your son/daughter treat your other children?

Secondary student's self-assessment of educational profile

Name: ....

1. Which aspects of reading do you enjoy and find easy in school and out of school?

2. Which aspects of reading do you consider you need to improve to obtain higher marks?

3. Which aspects of writing do you find easy?

4. Which aspects of writing would you like to improve?

5. Which aspects of spelling do you find easy?

6. Which aspects of spelling do you find hard?

7. Which aspects of mathematics do you find easy?

8. Which aspects of mathematics do you find hard?

9. Do you enjoy participating in group discussion?

10. Do you enjoy answering questions in class?

11. Are you happy with your progress/performance in all your school subjects?

12. Do you consider yourself to be well behaved in school?

13. How do you treat teachers?

14. How do you treat other pupils?

15. How do you treat other people's property?

16. Do you have any eyesight, hearing or speech problems?

17. How would you describe your memory?

18. What do you find easy to remember?

19. What do you find difficult to remember?

20. How do you remember what you have learnt in lessons?

21. How would you describe your organisational skills?

22. What are the subjects you enjoy and are good at in school and outside school?

23. Which subjects do you consider need improving in school?

24. Under what circumstances do you produce poor quality written work?

Suggestions for motivating secondary students to learn

As motivation plays a large part in effective learning the following are a few suggestions to motivate and encourage positive attitudes.

1. Try to get the answers you want from the students by asking carefully phrased and structured questions. This allows students to provide answers which you can build on during the lesson.
2. Give concrete examples of how knowledge gained from your lesson could benefit them. Encourage them to think of how knowledge from your lessons could be of use in the future.
3. Always be well prepared and organised, have spare work available which can be adapted for different abilities.
4. Pass favourable comments in front of the class to those who are displaying positive attitudes to their work especially to those who are least likely to expect it. Similarly, show the class good examples of written work which you would like produced. Model examples on the board if necessary.
5. Try to present your teaching material in as many different forms as possible and try to bring your teaching to life. To sustain interest try to obtain as much of the following as you can: a range of textbooks, videos on the subject, posters, invite a visitor who is an expert, arrange an out of school visit, bring in concrete objects to be displayed. Where possible adopt a cross-curricular approach to imparting knowledge to students as there is a greater chance of their memory and understanding being reinforced.
6. Think of activities, whereby, all the students are actively participating and contributing to the lesson, many students remember and understand through experiencing and 'living' their education.
7. Aim to promote a sense of success and boost all the student's self-confidence by finding something different and worthwhile to say about each student's contribution to the lesson. It is important to say how a student's work is valued and could be improved.
8. Give responsibility to secondary students who have low self-esteem.
9. Peer approval can be confidence building – students can be encouraged to be complimentary about each other's work. For example, working in pairs students could swap written work and share with the class its positive qualities.
10. Provide interesting handouts – use a font or typeface which is slightly larger than normal which can be easily read, include illustrations to appeal to visual learners, make sure your handout has clear subheadings to guide the learner's understanding.
11. If you need students to copy anything from the whiteboard/blackboard prepare the board before the class begins. Stand at the back of the class to make sure that it can be easily seen and read. The use of alternate colours on the blackboard/whiteboard is a practical tip which assists student's hand and eye coordination.

2 Practical assessment approaches for secondary students

Chapter 2 follows on from the initial assessment approaches outlined in Chapter 1 by focusing on formal and informal approaches to identify dyslexia in secondary students. Detailed information is provided about formal assessment tests available and a variety of informal assessment approaches are described. These include three worksheets, 'Getting to know you', 'Self-assessment of English' and 'Pupil–peer observation worksheet', to assist subject teachers in becoming familiar with a student's strengths and limitations at the start of the academic year. Other informal methods of assessment include the use of active listening techniques and a checklist to discover if a student's diet is affecting their academic work. The chapter ends with two examples of assessment of students' written work with suggestions for improvement.

Formal and informal assessment approaches should be administered with the SENCO's full knowledge and approval to discover a secondary student's educational requirements. Once these are known it is possible to reflect upon which teaching strategies and resources can be used to develop specific study skills. Practical guidance is to be found in Chapters 5, 6, and 7.

Schools' Survey

Kindly list the assessment techniques, strategies, methods and resources used by your school to discover dyslexia in secondary students.

Responses to this request revealed that the following approaches were used to identify and assess dyslexia in secondary students:

- *assessments by the Learning and Behaviour Support Services;*
- *informal teacher observations and formal testing;*
- *the use of parental concerns;*
- *the use of various tests: Aston Index, Wisc Tests, Bangor Dyslexia Test, Macmillan Reading Test, Schonell Spelling Test, British Picture Vocabulary Scale (BPVS), Ravens Progressive Matrices, Psychologists' test (British Ability Scales – BAS) Cognitive Ability Test, Wide Range Achievement Test;*
- *Reading Age and Spelling Age;*
- *previous school records;*
- *visual, auditory, diagnostic and phonological tests;* and
- *free writing and reading and comprehension analysis.*

Formal diagnostic tests used for the assessment of dyslexia in secondary schools

Formal diagnostic tests to determine dyslexia in secondary students should only ever be administered by SENCOs in schools. Information regarding such tests is given in Table 2.1. Resources marked *** are tests which can be used to obtain GCSE and A Level examination concessions. Implications arising from diagnostic tests should always be related to students' personal and curriculum needs and considered alongside informal assessments.

Addresses and contact information were correct at the time of publication, but readers are advised to make allowances for subsequent changes.

Table 2.1 Formal diagnostic tests for the assessment of dyslexia

Name of test, function and completion time	Contents	Age group and suitability (group or individual use)	Suppliers
Aston Index 16 tests assess ability in reading, spelling, auditory and visual sequential memory, graphmotor, vocabulary scale, sound blending, and sound discrimination. Time: varies according to test undertaken	Comprehensive battery of 16 tests for screening and diagnosing language difficulties. Provides complete profile of ability and attainment in different skill areas. 17 test cards, box of support materials, 30 score-sheets, photocopiable test sheet. Instruction manual included	Age range: 5–14 Test: individual	**LDA** Duke Street, Wisbech, Cambs PE13 2AE Tel: 01945 463441 FAX: 01945 587361 email: ldaorders@ compuserve.com **Better Books** 3 Paganel Drive, Dudley, West Midlands DY1 4AZ Tel: 01384 253276 **Hornsby Centre** Wye Street, London SW11 2HB Tel: 020 7223 1144 FAX: 020 7924 1112 email: dyslexia@ hornsby.co.uk **SEN Marketing** 18 Leeds Rd, Outwood, Wakefield WF1 2LT Tel/FAX: 01924 871697 email: sen.marketing@ ukonline.co.uk

Table 2.1 *cont.*

Name of test, function and completion time	Contents	Age group and suitability (group or individual use)	Suppliers
Bangor Dyslexia Test Screens for 10 dyslexia-type difficulties. Easily administered oral test. Time: 15–20 minutes	A5 score-sheets in A4 plastic wallet and instruction booklet	Age range: 8–adult Test: individual	**LDA** Duke Street, Wisbech, Cambs PE13 2AE Tel: 01945 463441 FAX: 01945 587361 email: ldaorders@ compuserve.com **Better Books** 3 Paganel Drive, Dudley, West Midlands DY1 4AZ Tel: 01384 253276 **SEN Marketing** 18 Leeds Rd, Outwood, Wakefield WF1 2LT Tel/FAX: 01924 871697 email: sen.marketing@ ukonline.co.uk
British Picture Vocabulary Scale (BPVS)***, 2nd edn A verbal comprehension test which is easily administered. Only oral responses are required to picture cards. Time: Up to 15 minutes	168 test items, test book, 2 packs of record forms, supplement for EFL pupils, guide, carry case. Instructions included	Age range: 3–15.8 Test: individual	**NFER-Nelson** Darville House, 2 Oxford Road East, Windsor, Berks SL4 1DF Tel: 01753 858961 FAX: 01753 856830 email: edu&hsc@ nfer-nelson.co.uk
British Spelling Tests (BSTS)*** 5 level spelling tests, each with 2 parallel forms, using a variety of methods – individual word dictation, proofreading and error detection. Time: About 30 to 40 minutes	Specimen set containing a manual, test booklet and an at-a-glance guide. Each of the 5 levels has its own starter set	Age range: 5 to adult BSTS 1:5 to 8.11 BSTS 2:7 to 11.11 BSTS 3:9 to 15.1 BSTS 4:12.6 to 17.5 BSTS 5:15.6 upwards (including adults) Test: group or individual	**NFER-Nelson** Darville House, 2 Oxford Road East, Windsor, Berks SL4 1DF Tel: 01753 858961 FAX: 01753 856830 email: edu&hsc@ nfer-nelson.co.uk

Table 2.1 *cont.*

Name of test, function and completion time	Contents	Age group and suitability (group or individual use)	Suppliers
Cognitive Abilities Test (CAT) *** Measures verbal, quantitative and non-verbal reasoning ability. Recognises students who are underachieving by comparing ability with attainment; enables the setting of realistic achievement targets. Time: 40 minutes Practice Test: 55 minutes for each ability area	Specimen set of administration manual, a pupil's profile and a group linear profile. Pupil booklet and practice test with answer sheets, separate pack needed for each level. Set of two scoring overlays, separate set needed for each level	Age range: 7.6–15.9 Levels A,B,C 8–11 Levels D, E, and F 12–14+ Level D is widely used in screening on entry to secondary school Test: group	**NFER-Nelson** Darville House, 2 Oxford Road East, Windsor, Berks SL4 1DF Tel: 01753 858961 FAX: 01753 856830 email: edu&hsc@ nfer-nelson.co.uk
Edinburgh Reading Tests*** To determine student's reading competency in different areas. Tests reveal both student's reading strengths and limitations. Time: Stage 1: (7–9 yrs) 2 sessions lasting 25 minutes Stages 2 and 3 (Stage 2: 8.6–10.6 yrs Stage 3: 10–12.6 yrs) require 3 sessions lasting 40 minutes. New restandardised Stage 4: (11.7–14.6 yrs) requires 1 session lasting 45 minutes	There are four levels of reading depending on the age group. Each level is composed of four or more individually timed sub-tests assessing a different reading component. Instructions provided	Age range: 7–14.6 Test: group or individual	**Hodder & Stoughton** Bookpoint Ltd, 78 Milton Park, Abingdon, Oxon OX14 4TD Tel: 02078 736000 FAX: 01235 400454 email: orders@ bookpoint.co.uk **SEN Marketing** 18 Leeds Rd, Outwood, Wakefield WF1 2LT Tel/FAX: 01924 871697 email: sen.marketing@ ukonline.co.uk
Lucid Assessment System for School (LASS) A computerised multi-functional assessment system. Automatic scoring system. Time: 30–45 minutes	Assesses intelligence, reading, spelling, memory and phonological ability using CD-ROMs.	Age range: 11–15 years Test: individual (easy for teachers to implement and students to administer)	**Lucid Creative Limited** PO Box 63 Beverley, East Yorkshire HU17 8ZZ Tel: 01482 465589

Table 2.1 *cont.*

Name of test, function and completion time	Contents	Age group and suitability (group or individual use)	Suppliers
	Contains 7 modules which can be used separately or in combination allowing teachers to: measure progress in memory, phonological and phonic skills; monitor development in reading and spelling regularly; identify dyslexia; measure discrepancies between actual and expected literacy attainment; assess the student's attainments in reading and spelling; and obtain a reasonable estimation of the student's intelligence. Demonstration disks available on request. Instructions included		email: inso@ lu-research.com
NFER **New Reading Analysis** This test provides oral reading accuracy and comprehension scores, diagnostic information on reading strategies, and allows miscue analysis.	An individual verbal reading test providing a selection of 6 graded passages with comprehension questions on each.	Age range: 7.5–13; Reading Age equivalents provided from 5.8 to 12.4 Test: individual	**NFER-Nelson** Darville House, 2 Oxford Road East, Windsor, Berks SL4 1DF Tel: 01753 858961 FAX: 01753 856830 email: edu&hsc@

Table 2.1 *cont.*

Name of test, function and completion time	Contents	Age group and suitability (group or individual use)	Suppliers
Particularly suitable for diagnosis and assessment. Three parallel forms (A, B, C) allow re-testing without familiarity. Time: 15 minutes	Starter manual, 1 reading booklet, 3 packs (25 record sheets each for forms A, B, C)		nfer-nelson.co.uk
Phonological Assessment Battery (PhAB)* by Frederickson, Frith and Reason. The following are assessed individually: alliteration, naming speed (picture naming, digit naming), rhyme, spoonerisms, fluency and non-word reading. This test assesses phonological skills, provides a profile, offers specific suggestions for IEP planning and teaching activities and is easy to use. Time: 30–40 minutes	Complete set of manual and 10 record forms. Sample sheets which provide the rationale behind the assessment to determine its suitability in school. Instruction manual included	Age range: 6–14.11 Test: individual	**NFER-Nelson** Darville House, 2 Oxford Road East, Windsor, Berks SL4 1DF Tel: 01753 858961 FAX: 01753 856830 email: edu&hsc@ nfer-nelson.co.uk
Ravens Progressive Matrices* This test assesses non-verbal reasoning and is not timed. 3 levels: • Easy – coloured progressive matrices, Crichton Vocabulary Scale 5 – 11+ • Average – standard progressive matrices, Mill Hill Vocabulary Scale (junior form 11–adult) • Difficult – advanced progressive matrices, Mill Hill Vocabulary Scale (senior form FE, HE, post-grad' entry to employment)	Specimen sets of: • coloured progressive matrices • standard progressive matrices • advanced progressive matrices (Specimen set contains one relevant copy of the book of tests each for sets 1 and 11, a manual section for the relevant matrices, and one record form)	Age range: 5–adult Test: group or individual	**NFER-Nelson** Darville House, 2 Oxford Road East, Windsor, Berks SL4 1DF Tel: 01753 858961 FAX: 01753 856830

Table 2.1 *cont.*

Name of test, function and completion time	Contents	Age group and suitability (group or individual use)	Suppliers
Time: varies according to test – average about 30 minutes	Crichton Vocabulary Scale – record form, (pack of 10) Mill Hill Vocabulary Scale – definitions form (pack of 20) record form (pack of 20)		
Richmond Test of Basic Skills Provides a comprehensive profile of pupils' attainment in vocabulary, spelling, punctuation, study skills and mathematics. 6 levels, one year each: 1 to 3 primary; 4, age 11–12; 5, age 12–13; 6, age 13–14. Time: Varies to the test being given	Specimen set which includes an administration manual, pupil's book, Level 1, answer sheet, class record sheet, pupil profile chart, circular profile Pupil book Pack of 25 answer sheets for each level Scoring overlays for each level	Age range: 8–14 Test: group	**NFER-Nelson** Darville House, 2 Oxford Road East, Windsor, Berks SL4 1DF Tel: 01753 858961 FAX: 01753 856830 email: edu&hsc@ nfer-nelson.co.uk
Vernon Graded Word SpellingTest* To determine spelling age and ability of students. Time: 20–30 minutes	80 word spelling test, based on Macmillan Spelling Series. This test is easy to administer and mark. Includes instruction handbook	Age range: scores from 6.1 to 17.6+ Test: group or individual	**Hodder & Stoughton** Bookpoint Ltd, 78 Milton Park, Abingdon, Oxon OX14 4TD Tel: 02078 736000 FAX: 01235 400454 email: orders@ bookpoint.co.uk **SEN Marketing** 18 Leeds Rd, Outwood, Wakefield

Table 2.1 *cont.*

Name of test, function and completion time	Contents	Age group and suitability (group or individual use)	Suppliers
			WF1 2LT Tel/FAX: 01924 871697 email: sen.marketing@ ukonline.co.uk
Beery-Buktenica Development Test of Visual-Motor Integration (VM1)* A quick and effective resource for identifying visual-motor difficulties. Test: 15 minutes approximately	Students have to copy geometric figures as accurately as possible. Two versions available: a Short Record Form (containing 15 figures suitable for children aged 3 to 6), and a Long Record Form (with 24 figures, can be used up to 18 years and beyond), with two optional tests which evaluate visual perception and motor coordination in relation to VM1 performance. Includes instructions	Age range: 3–18+ Test: group or individual	**Ann Arbor** P.O. Box 1, Bedford Northumberland NE70 7JX Tel: 01668 214460 FAX: 01668 214484 email: enquiries@ annarbor.co.uk **NFER-Nelson** Darville House, 2 Oxford Road East, Windsor, Berks SL4 1DF Tel: 01753 858961 FAX: 01753 856830 email: edu&hsc@ nfer-nelson.co.uk
Wordchains* A timed word reading test which can identify dyslexia comprises two parts: 1. Letterchains – identifies visual motor dysfunction, consists of clusters of letters presented in the form of 90 chains of 3 or 4 clusters. The task is to divide as many clusters as possible within 3 minutes.	Specimen set containing the manual and one pupil booklet Starter set containing the manual and 20 pupil booklets Pupil booklets	Age range: 7–adult Test: group or individual	**NFER-Nelson** Darville House, 2 Oxford Road East, Windsor, Berks SL4 1DF Tel: 01753 858961 FAX: 01753 856830 email: edu&hsc@ nfer-nelson.co.uk

Table 2.1 *cont.*

Name of test, function and completion time	Contents	Age group and suitability (group or individual use)	Suppliers
2. Wordchains – The task is to divide 4000 nouns, verbs and adjectives familiar to the early reader within 3 minutes. Time: Letterchains – 90 secs Wordchains – 3 mins			
Wide Range Achievement Test WRAT*** This publication is extensively used in schools and assesses reading, spelling and numeracy. Time: varies according to test	Single word reading and spelling; numeracy; 2 parallel forms. Instruction manual included	Age range: 5–75 Test: group or individual	**The Psychological Corporation** High Street, Foots Cray, Sidcup, Kent DA14 5HP Tel: 02083 085750 email: tpc@harcourt.com **Dyslexia Institute** 133 Greshams Road, Staines, Middlesex TW18 2AJ Tel: 01784 463851 email: info@ dyslexia-inst.org.uk

Informal methods to assess dyslexia in secondary students

It is advisable that the SENCO is kept fully informed throughout the process of informal assessment approaches in the secondary school. We may ask ourselves what are the informal methods to identify dyslexia in secondary students? Basically, it comes down to making sense of detailed observational knowledge gathered from all those who are involved and care about secondary students. Like detectives, teachers gather and uncover meaningful evidence which unlocks students' potential. At the start of every academic year teachers need to get to know their students. The following three worksheets provide teachers with information for lesson planning. They have the flexibility of being suitable for a whole class or individual use. The worksheets entitled 'Getting to know you' could be used across the curriculum as could the 'Pupil–peer observation worksheet'.

This worksheet may provide teachers with an insight into aspects of the pupil of which teachers may previously have been unaware.

Getting to know you

Name: ....

List the subjects and skills you are good at both inside and outside school.

List your least favourite subjects in and outside school.

What is it you wish to gain from your education in school?

What do you like most about your education in school?

What do you find most difficult in school and why?

How do you like to be taught in school? (Tick the following methods which reflect the way in which you like to work in class.)

Listening to explanations given by the teacher ☐
Using a textbook with the teacher's guidance ☐
Working on your own in class ☐
Working with a partner ☐
Working in a group ☐
The use of the blackboard/whiteboard during lessons ☐
The use of demonstrations using real objects ☐
Class discussions ☐
Other (explain in your own words) ☐

What is your behaviour like during lessons?

Tick Yes or No to each of the following questions: Yes No

Do you arrive in class fully organised with the correct books,
pens, and paper for lessons? ☐ ☐
Are you easily distracted during lessons? ☐ ☐
Do you listen in class? ☐ ☐
Do you understand what the teacher says in class? ☐ ☐
Are you willing to work in school? ☐ ☐

Which resources do you think improve your understanding and performance in academic subjects? (Tick those you like.)

textbooks ☐
fiction books ☐
dictionaries ☐
computers ☐
television ☐
videos ☐
CD-ROMs ☐
cassette tapes ☐
overhead projectors (OHPs) ☐
the use of teacher handouts ☐
other (please list) ....

Secondary student's self-assessment of English

Name: ....

	Yes	No
Are you good at reading?	☐	☐
Do you find it easy to understand what you read?	☐	☐
Can you use the knowledge gained from your reading in different situations?	☐	☐
Do you find it easy to read silently?	☐	☐
Do you find it takes a long time to read?	☐	☐
Do you read a lot?	☐	☐
Do you find essay writing easy?	☐	☐
Do you find it easy to spell new difficult words?	☐	☐
Is your handwriting good?	☐	☐
Do you have good listening skills?	☐	☐
Do you find it easy to remember what you have learnt?	☐	☐
Do you find English easy?	☐	☐
Do you know how to use a dictionary?	☐	☐
Do you know how to use the library for research?	☐	☐
Can you improve your reading, writing and spelling skills?	☐	☐

Pupil–peer observation worksheet

Name of pupil observer: ....

Name of pupil being observed: ....

Tick the answer which applies to ....(name of pupil being observed)

	Yes	No
Can they work well on their own?	☐	☐
Do they work well in a group?	☐	☐
Are they easily distracted?	☐	☐
Do they finish all the work set in a lesson?	☐	☐
Do they find it easy to follow instructions?	☐	☐
Do they find it easy to remember what has been taught?	☐	☐
Do they find it easy to write essays?	☐	☐
Do you think they contribute well to class discussions?	☐	☐
Do they make many spelling mistakes?	☐	☐
Are they well organised for lessons?	☐	☐
Are they well behaved during lessons?	☐	☐
Do they have a good attitude towards their work?	☐	☐

List the subjects they are good at in school: ....

....

....

....

....

....

....

Checklist for subject teacher's assessment of organisational and social skills, written work, reading and speaking and listening skills and physical and emotional factors

Name of teacher: ....Date: ....

Name of pupil: ....Year: ....

Known strengths:

Existing limitations:

Skills	Yes/No	Other information
Organisational skills Is properly organised for lessons?		
Finishes the work which has been set?		
Always checks work thoroughly?		
Can work independently?		
Can complete homework properly?		
Social skills Finds it easy to mix with other students?		
Has a good attendance record?		
Likes to participate in class?		

Checklist for subject teacher's assessment of skills cont.

Skills	Yes/No	Other information
Tries to avoid working?		
Is well-behaved in class?		
Has respect for those in authority?		
Written work Handwriting is legible?		
Has good copying skills?		
Writes quickly?		
Ideas, thoughts expressed clearly in written work?		
Examination questions answered appropriately?		
Can spell specialised vocabulary across the curriculum?		
General spelling is good?		

© Marion Griffiths 2002. *Study Skills and Dyslexia in the Secondary School.* Published by David Fulton Publishers. ISBN: 1 85346 790 1

Checklist for subject teacher's assessment of skills cont.

Skills	Yes/No	Other information
Can write essays with confidence?		
Has good note-taking skills?		
Reading skills Can read and understand all texts across the curriculum?		
Can read and follow written instructions in essay questions?		
Likes reading?		
Finds it easy to conduct research for assignments and course work?		
Rarely misunderstands what he/she reads?		
Speaking and listening skills Is willing to participate in class discussions?		
Can express himself/herself coherently?		
Has good listening comprehension skills?		

© Marion Griffiths 2002. *Study Skills and Dyslexia in the Secondary School.* Published by David Fulton Publishers. ISBN: 1 85346 790 1

Checklist for subject teacher's assessment of skills cont.

Skills	Yes/No	Other information
Can follow instructions?		
Can remember and act upon instructions?		
Has mature language skills?		
Does not stammer, hesitate or stutter in speech?		
Never has difficulty finding the correct word to use in speech?		
Physical/emotional factors Has good coordination of fine motor skills and gross motor skills?		
Is able to hear accurately with both ears?		
Has good eyesight?		
Has psychological or emotional factors which hinder academic progress?		

© Marion Griffiths 2002. *Study Skills and Dyslexia in the Secondary School*. Published by David Fulton Publishers. ISBN: 1 85346 790 1

Active listening techniques for use with secondary students

Active listening techniques can facilitate good student–practitioner communication during individual teaching encounters. Secondary students' academic work and personal concerns can be explored in depth and also information can be gathered to benefit students in the future. Active listening techniques include:

1. Maintain good eye contact.
2. Make appropriate facial expressions to what is being said.
3. Show an interest in what the student says.
4. Be attentive to what is being said and how it is being said.
5. Be aware of non-verbal communication.
6. Analyse, monitor and reflect upon what has been said.
7. Encourage students to discuss, explore and find their own practical solutions to academic and non-academic issues.
8. Ask specific questions which will guide students towards increased self-awareness, self-discovery and realistic and manageable solutions.
9. Try and understand the student's world from his/her point of view.
10. Have positive regard and respect for the student.

Assessment of secondary students' health

While it is recognised that teachers are not health specialists general observations of students' physical well-being can be important during the teenage years. During adolescence some teenagers may have a poor self-image and may feel under pressure to diet. If students are allergic to foods learning could be affected. If a student answers yes to more than one of the questions outlined in the checklist below the teacher should advise the student to visit their general practitioner.

Checklist to discover if a student's diet affects academic work

	Yes	No
1. Has the student any known allergies to food?	☐	☐
2. Does the student's behaviour change after eating certain foods?	☐	☐
3. Is the student's work rate affected by eating or drinking certain foods?	☐	☐
4. Do any foods affect the student's concentration?	☐	☐
5. Is the student on a special diet for medical reasons which the school should know about and does it affect the student's education?	☐	☐
6. Does the student show signs of tiredness?	☐	☐

Assessing secondary students' written work with suggestions for improvement

In preparation for external examinations useful study skills are needed, for example, writing timed essays and knowledge of how to summarise information. The ability to summarise, that is extract key points from a short passage of text, can be useful across the curriculum for revision puposes, for writing conclusions and preparing essays. Two examples of assessing such written work are given here, a creative piece of writing and a summary of a short passage from *Pride and Prejudice*.

Creative writing

For GCSE English language examinations students are expected to produce creative essays. The following was written by a 14-year-old student who was asked to produce a timed essay entitled 'Alone in the house' in 20 minutes.

Alone in the house

It was a dark winter night and I was eating my tea which I had prepared for myself. Then I heard somebody walking in the snow just outside, so I ran to the window and look out. All I could see was a blue van with a man sitting in the passenger seat. Another man soon went to the van, but the other man got out with two crow bars. I now I had to do something.

I had to do something so I ran out the back door and got the tar from the shed and poured it all over the back door step then I closed the door. I ran around the house and locked all the windows then I left the front door unlocked with a bucket of paint over the top. Then I put a fan a few feet away from the door with a pile of feathers in front of it. I ran to my bedroom and get all the marbles and put them at the top of the stairs. I then close my mum's door and attached a cork board to it. Then I ran to my bedroom and found my bow and arrows and put them next to my door.

Then I jumped over the marbles and ran down the stairs. I look out of the window of the living room and saw the men coming. One man went to the back door and the other man went to the front door. The man who went to the back was stuck in the tar, then I had to fight the last of the two men, when he opened the front door the paint fell on him, I turned the tar on and shouted at him, I ran upstairs and got into position with my bow and arrows, I heard him running up the stairs and I fired arrows at him and he was stuck to the door. I picked up the phone in my room and called the police who turned up in minutes to arrest the men.
(349 words)

Suggestions for improvement

It is important to calculate the rate of words per minute produced by secondary students under timed conditions to discover whether examination concessions may be necessary. It is regarded that students need to produce an average of 15 words per minute for GCSE if, however, 12 words per minute or less are produced then it may be necessary to apply for 25 per cent extra time in examinations.

The above writer produced an average rate of 17 words per minute at the age of 14 so while his writing rate is just slightly above the average rate there is also time to for him to improve. He could increase his writing speed through regular practice of timed essays in all his curriculum subjects. It is strongly recommended that early on in secondary education, students routinely practise timed essays in preparation for later external examinations.

Suggestions for improvement of the above piece of writing:

- The strength of this piece of writing is that the content relates to the title indicating that the essay question has been answered. There is a recognisable structure with a definite beginning, middle and end. The text is fast moving and flows well in keeping with the story line. Conversation between the two burglars and more description of them throughout this piece of prose would have provided greater depth and meaning.The ending could have been expanded by including a reaction from the burglars when the police arrived to arrest them.
- The writer needs to revise paragraphs – the first sentence of the essay should be indented.
- There needs to be a thorough proofreading of the text. (The 'Checklist for students to improve the quality of written work' in Chapter 6 provides guidance for this.) The writer's frequent use of the incorrect tense needs to be specifically addressed and corrected here (for example '*look*' has been written instead of '*looked*' (lines 3 and 16). In line 5 the word '*now*' needs to be replaced with '*knew*'. The student also needs to be made aware of words which begin with a silent k. In line 12 '*got*' should have been written instead of '*get*', and '*closed*' should have written instead of '*close*' (line 13).
- There is much repetition of the connective word '*then*' throughout the text and alternative words need to be found after the first usage of this word, such as '*later*'. Alternatively a specification of time could be given when the next event occurred, for example instead of saying '*Then I jumped over the marbles and ran down the stairs*' the writer could have said '*Five minutes later I jumped over the marbles and ran down the stairs.*'
- The writer needs to transfer the literacy techniques outlined above to improve his writing in other curriculum subjects. For example he must remember to indent correctly at the beginning of paragraphs, use the correct tense and avoid repetitive usage of vocabulary and phrases.

Writing a summary

To establish a student's ability to summarise a short passage of text, Helen, a 15-year-old student, was asked to read the following extract from Chapter 46 of *Pride and Prejudice* by Jane Austen and produce a summary of what she had read. The student was given no indication as to how long the summary should be or how long it should take to write. The object of the exercise was to see what the student could do and produce.

> 'Oh! where, where is my uncle?' cried Elizabeth, darting from her seat as she finished the letter, in eagerness to follow him, without losing a moment of the time so precious; but as she reached the door, it was opened by a servant, and Mr Darcy appeared. Her pale face and impetuous manner made him start, and before he could recover himself enough to speak, she, in whose mind every idea was superseded by Lydia's situation, hastily exclaimed, 'I beg your pardon, but I must leave you. I must find Mr Gardiner, this moment, on business that cannot be delayed; I have not an instant to lose.'
>
> 'Good God! what is the matter?' cried he, with more feeling than politeness; then recollecting himself, 'I will not detain you a minute, but let me, or let the servant, go after Mr and Mrs Gardiner. You are not well enough; – you cannot go by yourself.'
>
> Elizabeth hesitated, but her knees trembled under her and she felt how little would be gained by her attempting to pursue them. Calling back the servant, therefore, she commissioned him, though in so breathless an accent as made her almost unintelligible, to fetch his master and mistress home, instantly.
>
> On his quitting the room, she sat down, unable to support herself, and looking so miserably ill, that it was impossible for Darcy to leave her; or to refrain from saying, in a tone of gentleness and commiseration, 'Let me call your maid. Is there nothing you could take, to give you present relief? – A glass of wine; – shall I get you one? – You are very ill.'
>
> 'No, I thank you;' she replied, endeavouring to recover herself. 'There is nothing the matter with me. I am quite well. I am only distressed by some dreadful news which I have just received from Longbourn.'
>
> She burst into tears as she alluded to it, and for a few minutes could not speak another word. Darcy, in wretched suspense, could only say something indistinctly of his concern, and observe her in compassionate silence. At length she spoke again. 'I have just had a letter from Jane, with such dreadful news. It cannot be concealed from any one. My youngest sister has left all her friends – has eloped; – has thrown herself into the power of Mr Wickham. They are gone off together from Brighton. *You* know him too well to doubt the rest. She has no money, no connections, nothing that can tempt him to – she is lost for ever.'
>
> (Austen 1813, extract from 1972 edition)

Helen's summary is as follows.

Pride and Prejudice – a summary of the extract by Jane Austen

The author of this passage recounts how upset Elizabeth is. She tells her friend Mr D'Arcy that her youngest sister Lydia is left home and married Mr Wickham.

Suggestions for improvement

Suggestions for improvement of Helen's summary:

- Helen's summary shows that she basically understood the text's content. The opening sentence ends with a verb which is not considered to be good English – it would have been an improvement to have written 'The author of this passage recounts how Elizabeth became upset.'
- Helen needs to briefly explain *why* and *how* Elizabeth became increasingly agitated at the thought of her sister's undesirable relationship with Mr Wickham. To do this, as she was reading the text, Helen could have asked herself – What was the main point of the paragraph and what was the author trying to show? To answer these questions, Helen could have highlighted key words and phrases from each paragraph which she could have rephrased in her summary. In the first and second paragraphs, Elizabeth, looks pale and desperately wants to tell her aunt and uncle the sad news from her letter. The affect of her youngest sister's actions become clearer in the third and fourth paragraphs. Elizabeth is on the point of fainting and finally bursts into tears as she tells Darcy. Helen needs to briefly explain the nature of Darcy's concern for Elizabeth in her summary.
- Helen needs to avoid careless copying errors from the text such as the misspelling of the word Darcy.
- Helen needs to proofread her work to check that she has used the correct tense. For example, the second sentence should read 'She tells her friend Mr *Darcy* that her youngest sister Lydia *has* left home and married Mr Wickham.'

3 Implementing a study skills programme following assessment

SENCOs and/or Learning Support Teachers can use the information provided by the assessments discussed in Chapters 1 and 2 to tailor a study skills programme to the individual needs of a particular student. Chapter 3 discusses the factors that should be taken into account when preparing such a programme. It is important to encourage students to be involved in their learning and examples of the academic targets that students aim to achieve after following a study skills programme are provided along with suggestions as to how these targets can be fulfilled. A case study of a student at Key Stage 3 (KS3) is used as the basis for demonstrating how a suitable study skills programme can be developed. The chapter concludes by addressing the issue of assessing and preparing students with dyslexia for GCSE examinations.

Factors to be considered when preparing a study skills programme

When preparing a study skills programme for a secondary learner with dyslexia the following factors should be taken into account:

- the study skills' needs and aims of the student should be identified and prioritised;
- a 'holistic' assessment of the student's strengths and limitations should be recorded to inform a study skills programme by collating assessment information as outlined in Chapters 1 and 2;
- the student should be taught study skills strategies which can be used across the curriculum;
- a variety of teaching methods and resources should be used to consolidate and develop the student's learning; and
- the student should be encouraged to take an active role and use their initiative in their learning.

At the beginning of a study skills programme it is important to spend time talking to learners to identify specific curriculum requirements and aims. A student's character and personality need to be taken into account when considering how a study skills programme is to be implemented. It is important to obtain a notion for the direction in which the student is being prepared. It may be possible to ascertain a student's career preference. Simultaneously, factors may come to light which prevent the student from reaching their desired objectives. These may need to be identified and addressed before the study skills programme commences. For example, there is no point expecting a student to undertake extensive reading, writing assignments or embarking on a revision programme if they cannot see properly. A visit to the optician would take priority.

Two key aspects need to be considered when preparing a study skills programme:

- the content of the programme; and
- how the programme will be delivered.

Content of the study skills programme

It is worthwhile considering the following:

- Detailed examination and analysis of the student's existing study skills can form the basis of a study skills programme which could lead to success. The study skills being considered here are: note-taking, organisation, effective reading, writing essays, memory, revision and examination techniques.
- It is also important to take into account that students do not learn or digest the content of lessons at the same rate, therefore a student may need to revisit some teaching points during a study skills programme. This may involve teaching the same subject more than once and adopting an innovative approach using different resources.

Delivery of the study skills programme

Once the study skills content has been determined attention can turn to how the student is going to be taught what they need to know. It is worthwhile considering the following questions:

- Will the student be tutored on a one-to-one basis? Or would it be more appropriate for the student to be taught with a small group of peers?
- Where will the study skills programme take place? Is there a classroom which is already set up to address the needs of secondary students with dyslexia which contains resources such as: a televison, computers, laptops, spellcheckers, dictionaries, videos, audio cassettes and books? Or will the study skills programme take place in a classroom which is used for other purposes which will involve pre-planning of resources?
- How is knowledge of the student's strengths going to be used to enhance the student's learning?
- How is knowledge of the student's preferred learning style going to affect the study skills programme? In other words, how does the student embarking on a study skills programme like to learn and like to be taught?

Some students may prefer learning through the senses by adopting a multi-sensory approach, while others may prefer learning by 'doing' or learning through experience. Whatever the case, careful and precise assimilation of all the student's information will be necessary to tailor a study skills programme to correspond with the student's individual needs.

- Which resources are going to be effective in developing the student's study skills? It is worth considering how, where and when resources are going to be used. Having access to as wide a range of resources as possible allows greater flexibility for adaption should the need arise and they can be used to inspire teachers to create teaching materials to meet individual needs.

Examples of how students' academic targets can be met

At the beginning of a study skills programme, it is worth discussing with students the precise academic achievements to be addressed. Here is a selection of students' responses to the question 'What do you aim to achieve by following a study skills programme?' together with suggestions of how they could fulfil their academic targets.

Roger's academic targets at 13 – *'I intend to achieve a few more 'A's in my academic work and especially in biology, physics, chemistry and if possible history, geography, English and maths. I aim to do well with lots of perseverance and organisation.'*
With the teacher's guidance Roger needs to decide how he could achieve 'A' grades in biology, physics, chemistry, history, geography, English and maths. Here the Learning Support Teacher needs to liaise with each of the subject teachers to discover which teaching methods and which topics need to be reinforced as part of his study skills programme.

Susan's academic targets at 14 – *'I think I am going well but I could improve certain skills. For instance, listening and concentration. I would also like to get higher effort grades. I will have to put in some more effort to start off the process of getting higher grades.'*
Susan needs ideas and strategies to improve her listening and concentration during lessons throughout the curriculum. Her subject teachers could sit her at the front of the class beside students who are not likely to distract her. She could also be encouraged to focus on what the teacher is saying by taking notes. During lessons she could be encouraged to actively participate, for example by giving oral summaries of the main teaching points. Different methods of keeping her involved throughout all the lessons in the curriculum need to be considered so that her attention is permanently focused.

Keith's academic targets at 15 – *'I really want to get good grades at GCSE. I can achieve this by revising more for the subjects that I am taking.'*
Keith is motivated to obtain good GCSE results and has identified that he needs to revise more. Through discussion with his Learning Support Teacher

he needs to be guided to have a manageable, adaptable and practical revision timetable during term time and holidays to meet his curricular and leisure requirements. Whenever he is revising he would be advised to:

- only study in short bursts (he will remember more that way rather than trying to cram in too much in one go);
- take regular breaks;
- eat well and get plenty of sleep;
- change subjects regularly so that he does not get bored;
- make sure that he has obtained good detailed lesson notes which can be reduced down to portable cards containing key words to be read in free time;
- allow plenty of time for revision of weaker subjects;
- find as many different ways as possible to check what he has learnt.

Carly's academic targets at 16 – *'I really do not think I am doing as well as I could. I want to get better grades in my biology because I do not think I am trying my best in this subject.'*
Carly has identified that she needs to improve her biology and feels that she is not performing to the best of her ability in this subject. Her lack of progress clearly concerns her so it is important to find out why she is not doing her best. The reasons she gives would be the starting point from which to build a successful outcome in her study skills programme.

Apart from encouraging students to identify their academic needs SENCOs and Learning Support Teachers need to liaise with subject teachers to ascertain the National Curriculum requirements to be addressed in each subject.

Schools' Survey

What factors does your school take into account when delivering a study skills programme as part of an Individual Education Plan for secondary learners with dyslexia?

Schools considered that the following factors should be included when delivering a study skills programme:

- *'Must be fun – must be voluntary – must have a variety of tasks';*
- *'The severity of the child's difficulties and his/her ability to manage such a programme';*
- *'Individual learning style';*
- *'Previous learning, outside agency reports, previous assessments, pupil comments, staff input, exams (GCSEs needed by pupils for future career)';*
- *'Make sure that study skills being delivered help the student achieve targets on their IEP';*
- *'Need to balance "missing lessons" with useful skills to be acquired. Need to share/support time across subjects as well as "study skills" ';*
- *'Level of need – some students need daily programmes others three times a week or less';*

- *'Some will need in class support, others will need withdrawal to an alternative course or separate programmes etc.'* and
- *'Examination techniques for the basis of study skills.'*

A 'holistic' approach to a student's study skills programme

Using the assessment techniques outlined in Chapters 1 and 2 data will have been gathered to offer an insight into the student's learning profile. In addition, it is worth examining all the student's exercise books to see if there are recurring themes which need to be addressed as part of a study skills programme. For example, there may be common words which are frequently misspelled, proofreading skills may need revision and the student may need help with clarifying written expression. Moreover, the quality of the student's own notes should be assessed and if necessary specific guidance should be given to improve the quality of note-taking skills (see chapter 5).

Study skills strategies which can be used across the curriculum

There is a group of basic skills which will enhance students' learning throughout the curriculum if they are proficient in them. These are: note-taking, organisation, effective reading, writing essays, memory and revision and examination techniques. The acquisition and practice of these core techniques applied to a study skills programme frequently leads to improvement of the learner's academic performance. Up to a point study skills can be taught, nevertheless, simultaneously students should be encouraged to discover new methods which work for them.

The use of teaching methods and resources in a study skills programme

Generally speaking, students are more likely to understand and learn if they are presented with a variety of interesting teaching methods and resources when learning new concepts. Teachers may find role play and teaching in a cross-curricular manner beneficial to a student's learning. The teacher's expertise is invaluable in the classroom, and subject teachers may identify which resources can be used to enhance learning. Many students may respond well to the use of educational games, television, videos, computers, tape recorders, CD-ROMs, OHPs, Powerpoint, the Internet, scanners, the use of voice recognition programs and laptop computers.

An example of study skills programme at KS3

A practical approach to preparing a study skills programme is illustrated through the following case study.

Mark

Background information

Thirteen-year-old Mark has just started his secondary education. He is interested in sport. Poor spelling and written expression are his dyslexia-type difficulties. Mark demonstrates average aptitude and ability in the following subjects: Spanish, physics, geography, and mathematics. The subjects which he finds challenging are: English, biology, music, French, chemistry, history, design and technology and art.

A summary of Mark's end of term report

Teachers made many observations about Mark's performance during the Summer term. His report showed that he tried hard in most subjects, although he could be distracted. Staff are aware that Mark has an uneven profile of learning within subjects throughout the curriculum and that he needs to set himself higher academic standards. He should adopt a pro-active approach to educational matters as this would enhance his grades. Mark has a habit of handing in homeworks after the given deadline suggesting a need for improvement in his organisational skills. He is a popular student in his year.

Results of Mark's assessments

Spoken skills
Mark speaks fluently using grammatically correct sentence structure. His language, intonation and diction are suitable for his age. He is able to express himself clearly and he is able to give a logical, structured account of texts he has read a few days previously. Comprehension exercises present him with difficulty as he finds it hard to process his thoughts in a coherent manner. His limited vocabulary needs to be developed.

Phonological awareness
Mark's knowledge of sound-symbol correspondence has been checked and this aspect of his work does not present him with difficulty. Although Mark understands the principle of syllables he lacks the ability to demonstrate the correct number of syllables in some long words. He understands rhyme and is able to give examples of words which rhyme. He understands alliteration and can give examples of it for example *'George gave Gertrude a gun.'*

Reading skills

Mark is able to read single words, give verbal explanations of words and use a dictionary. A miscue analysis of an extract from *Of Mice and Men* (Steinbeck 1937) revealed the following:

- he followed the text with his finger;
- for the word 'darkening' he said 'dark';
- for the word 'brilliant' he said 'brightened';
- he repeated the words 'to him';
- for the word 'right out in' he said 'right out of';
- he repeated the words 'we'll have'; and
- he exaggerated the pronunciation of 'figuring' by saying 'fig/ur/ing'. Here he used an alphabetic strategy, that is using his knowledge of alphabet names and sounds to pronounce an unknown word.

Mark finds placing a grey overlay on top of texts improves reading. Words appear clearer, more evenly spaced out allowing increased fluency with oral and sight reading. It is considered that he employs contextual cues supported by logographic strategies when attempting to read unknown words. Mistakes can also be made when he rushes the reading of a text.

At the time of assessment Mark's chronological age was 13.04 and his reading age using the Wide Range Achievement Test was 12.00. This area of reading underachievement needs to be addressed.

Writing skills

There are many aspects of Mark's written work which need addressing. Poor spelling consistently mars the written work he produces – for example he wrote 'loanly' for lonely, and 'anougher' for another. He appears to use phonetic strategies for spelling such as, 'scarred' for scared, 'cumon' for come on, and 'lissen' for listen. He produces a neat, cursive script at a reasonable rate. His work is not sufficiently detailed to be acceptable at English KS3. He needs to improve his proofreading skills and punctuation. Written evidence has shown that he can produce a structured account of reading matter in his own words. He makes careless copying errors from OHPs and the blackboard. Punctuation presents him with a problem, namely using apostrophes incorrectly and forgetting to place full stops at the end of sentences. He needs to master the art of processing key information in comprehension exercises. He understands and knows how to use a dictionary correctly to enhance his work. He is right-handed and adopts a good posture when writing.

At the time of assessment Mark's chronological age was 13.04 whereas, his spelling age using the Wide Range Achievement Test was 10.05. His spelling potential must be realised.

Mathematical skills

Mark has mastered basic skills of counting, understanding place value, the meaning of mathematical symbols and the four rules of numbers. He has had difficulty understanding ratios and percentages.

Information from other sources

The Bangor Dyslexia Test (Miles 1983) suggested that Mark could be mildly dyslexic as he scored five positive factors out of ten. He volunteered the information that he lacked confidence at differentiating between his left hand and his right hand when he was younger, a skill which he had not completely acquired. He was unable to pronounce the polysyllabic word 'preliminary'. He demonstrated difficulty at manipulating number by his inability to give correct answers to mental subtraction sums and his inability to recite his 6, 7 and 8 times tables accurately by rote. His difficulty with sequencing was borne out by the fact that he was unable to say the months of the year in reverse order. There were indicators to suggest that he may have difficulty with his auditory sequential memory as he was unable to repeat series of numbers accurately forwards and backwards.

A summary of Mark's strengths and limitations

Strengths

The following points are considered to be Mark's strengths at the time of assessment:

- he works well in a one-to-one situation;
- he speaks clearly and accurately;
- his writing is legible and he is aware of sentence construction;
- he can write a structured account of what he has read;
- he can write at a reasonable rate;
- he has good rhyming ability and can understand how to use alliteration;
- he is making sound progress in Spanish, geography, physics and mathematics;
- he is able to read single words and give meanings for them;
- English is his first language and he is able to follow instructions;
- in a one-to-one situation his listening comprehension ability is good;
- his oral expression is acceptable for a student of his age and he is able to give a good logical structured account of what he read a few days previously;
- he does not make grammatical errors in speech; and
- he is progressing well in mathematics;

Limitations

The following points are considered to be Mark's limitations at the time of assessment:

- he has a poor memory;
- he is easily distracted in the class situation;
- he takes a passive view towards learning;
- he has poor organisational skills;
- he has difficulty identifying the number of syllables in words;
- he finds spelling difficult;

- he finds it difficult processing key information from comprehension exercises, answering comprehension exercises in sufficient detail and presenting the information in an acceptable written form;
- his proofreading skills are poor; and
- he has difficulty using punctuation correctly.

Information provided by assessment of a student such as Mark would form the basis for the SENCO and/or Learning Support Teacher to develop a study skills programme tailored to suit the individual's needs. Once such a study skills programme is prepared copies of it should be passed to subject teachers, who in turn can offer worthwhile feedback to SENCOs and Learning Support Teachers. The details of a possible programme, to suit a student with needs like those of Mark, will now be discussed.

The student would follow the programme with his or her Learning Support Teacher in two one-hour lessons each week during term time. The objectives of such a study skills programme would be as follows:

- to improve the student's English at KS3 and to provide the student with skills which can be used in other curriculum subjects; and
- to prepare the student for end of term examinations.

These two objectives would run concurrently throughout the term to address the student's study skills needs. As with most schemes the programme would be flexible because outside factors frequently determine the content of lessons. For example, there may be specific requests from subject teachers to concentrate on particular skills or there may be changes to the school timetable.

A KS3 English programme to reinforce and underpin mainstream English lessons

To develop a student's reading and writing to KS3 level an English programme designed to reinforce the mainstream English lessons could be followed. The rationale for this is twofold: reading comprehension plays a significant part of the KS3 English syllabus; and the ability to summarise a passage of text is a useful study skill particularly for revision purposes.

The student could be given the book *Of Mice and Men* by John Steinbeck (1937) which contains seven chapters, and each week he could be expected to read a chapter and to write a summary of it in 300 words. To assist the student the following advice on writing a summary would be provided.

Points to remember when writing a summary

- Read the text several times to make sure it is understood. Look up any unknown words in a dictionary and add them to your personal dictionary.
- Use a highlighting pen to identify the main point of a paragraph. The main point is normally found in the first sentence. Highlight other key words or phrases in subsequent sentences.

- Use a dictionary/thesaurus as an aid to finding alternative words/ phrases from the text.
- If possible write a first draft of the summary in pencil as this allows for later improvements and revisions.
- Make sure that the summary is shorter than the original as a summary is a condensed version of the main points contained within the text.
- Write the summary in your own words (don't just copy parts of the original).

The most common pitfalls that students make when writing summaries are that they retell the whole extract in their own words or copy large extracts from the text. To assist the process the student could be given an opportunity to watch a video of the book and in the eighth week the student could be asked to write a book review (see 'Book review worksheet' in Chapter 6).

Using different types of texts could provide the student with the opportunity to attempt comprehension exercises at different levels: literal, interpretative, critical and creative. Suggested texts for this are: *The Secret Diary of Adrian Mole aged 13³/₄* by Sue Townsend (1982), *The Machine Gunners* by Robert Westall (1975) and 'A night in a cottage' a short story by Richard Hughes (1989). At the end of the term the student could be given English KS3 practice papers, including essay questions, from which to work.

To develop comprehension skills throughout the curriculum the following teaching strategies and approaches could be used.

- The student should be encouraged to discuss their comprehension needs throughout the curriculum on a regular basis. To identify areas of difficulty specific comprehension strengths and limitations should be recorded.
- Before a text is studied an effort should be made to relate the student's personal knowledge and experience to that text. For example, discussion could take place about diaries prior to reading *The Secret Diary of Adrian Mole aged 13³/₄* (Townsend 1982).
- To check the student has understood a text they should be encouraged to give an oral account of what they have read in their own words.
- There should be close liaison between the SENCO, Learning Support Teacher, Learning Support Assistant (LSA), subject teachers and parents to address the student's comprehension needs.

Suggested resources for use in an English KS3 study skills programme

Arkin, A. and Sillars, S. (1993) *Spelling Rules OK!* Milton Keynes: Prontoprint Barking and The Modern Printers.
Brand, V. (1990) *Put it Right Copymasters.* Baldock, Herts.: Egon. (60 proofreading passages for use with 'remedial spelling' available from SEN Marketing, Better Books and Read and Write Educational Supplies – see Useful addresses)

Burt, A. (1990) *A Guide to Better Grammar.* Exmouth: Stanley Thornes.

Burt, A. (1991) *A Guide to Better Punctuation.* Exmouth: Stanley Thornes.

Burt, A. (1991) *A Guide to Better Spelling.* Exmouth: Stanley Thornes.

Hornsby, B. and Shear, F. (1980) *Alpha to Omega: The A to Z of teaching reading, writing and spelling – Stage 3, 13–15.* London: Heinemann.

Lisle, J. and Chadfield, J. (1997) *Practise and Prepare for Key Stage 3 National Tests – English.* London: Letts Educational.

Press, D. and McMamley, P. (1991) *Revision for Key Stage 3 with Answers.* London: John Murray.

KS3 English CD-ROM from WH Smith

Strategies to improve literacy skills

Literacy skills are required across the curriculum so time spent on improving them is worthwhile. A variety of strategies can be employed to this end, including encouraging the student to:

- Count or tap the beat of syllables of words as they are pronounced.
- Use a personal dictionary to write specialised words from the curriculum together with their meanings. (Use the books outlined above in the resources list to address specific spelling needs.)
- Undertake paired reading with a friend, whereby the partners can take it in turns to read to each other. Initially each partner could read alternate paragraphs extending to reading alternate pages until eventually the student may have the confidence to read a text to the whole class.
- Use a highlighting pen for comprehension exercises to identify relevant information from the text that could be used in a particular answer. The student could then be encouraged to reiterate the highlighted information in their own words and in preparation of writing the answer say it under their breath (subvocalise it) to check it makes sense. A tape recorder can be useful on these occasions, for example the LSA could record the student's oral attempts at answering the question and once an appropriate answer is given play the tape back to assist the student in transcribing it. Such a technique is useful in English language, English literature, history, geography, religious education (RE) and foreign languages.
- Practise writing summaries by using texts that interest the student. For example in the case study Mark was keen on sport so he could be asked to write a summary of a report of a particular sports match. Another exercise might involve him writing a commentary of a sporting event he has been shown on video.
- Learn how to spell five new words each week. It is easier if these five words come from a word family (e.g. words ending in 'ed' – replied, answered, responded, screamed and yelled).
- Use visualisation techniques to master the spelling of new and difficult words. Visualisation involves associating the new word with a familiar shape, colour, feeling or experience – personalising the word so it becomes easier to remember. So the student should ask themselves: What do they picture when they first hear the new word? and What does the shape of the

word remind them of? Such techniques can be used across the curriculum for learning new vocabulary associated with particular subjects.

- Always check their written work. The student should get into the habit of reading their work over, checking that it makes sense and being critical of it to see how and where improvements can be made. In exams the student should allow plenty of time to check their work thoroughly.
- Revise punctuation skills by completing proofreading exercises (e.g. Put it Right Copymasters – see resources list). Students could be given newspaper articles, poems, extracts from fiction and non-fiction and asked to justify why the author has used the punctuation in a particular way.

Strategies to prepare for end of term examinations

Preparations for end of tem examinations involve ensuring that the student is well organised and showing them how to tackle revision.

Strategies to improve daily organisational skills

These could include encouraging the student to:

- Make several copies of their timetable so that the information regarding what books and equipment they need each day at school and at home for homework is readily available. For example a student should have a copy of their timetable in their school bag, a second copy in their pocket, a third one at home in a prominent place in the kitchen so that the student's family can remind them every day of what they need and a final copy in the place where they study. Each copy of the timetable should be marked with the subject(s) given for homework on each particular night
- Be punctual for lessons and appointments. If the student has a watch that includes a timer function this could be set for particular lesson times.
- Monitor their daily organisational skills. For example, did they arrive on time for lessons? Did they have the correct books? Did they do the correct homework and was it handed in on time? The student should compare each day and each week's progress.
- Take a pride in each subject file across the curriculum. Notes taken in lessons are a gateway to future academic and career success – they represent the knowledge that must be understood and used in examinations. They need to be detailed, organised in a logical manner and looked after as they are likely to be referred to time and time again. Subject teachers should check lesson notes periodically, to ensure that they meet the required standard. The student should be shown how to keep notes in an organised way, for example by keeping a record of the topics in the front of each subject file, using plastic wallets and file dividers for subdividing topics within subjects (see Chapter 6 for note-taking skills).

Strategies for revision

From the beginning of term the student should be encouraged to:

- Spend 20 minutes each night revising a subject, a different subject being selected each night. The student must ensure that the relevant textbooks and exercise books are taken home to assist study.
- Use the list of topics in the front of each subject file as a checklist for revision.
- Monitor their progress by adopting a pro-active approach to learning by reading the text and underlining words or concepts that they don't understand so that they can try to find solutions to these academic difficulties (see Chapter 4). The student should then write out the main points of the newly acquired knowledge, record how long this takes and then check against the original text that all the key information is included.
- Inform teachers as soon as possible if they are experiencing difficulty with understanding a subject or topic within a subject. Equally staff should be aware of the student's educational needs and anticipate areas the student may find hard (see Chapter 4).

Once the student is given their exam timetable they should revise subjects in the order in which the exams will take place.

It should be made clear to the student that it is important to keep attention focused on the revision task during periods of study. Keeping focused can be aided by the following techniques:

- Using a highlighting pen to identify key words from texts.
- Making a note of questions that could be asked about the information being revised.
- Thinking of practical examples of how and where the information could be used.
- Thinking of other ways the information could be represented to assist understanding and recall later. Personalising new knowledge and information can help students retain it, for example use of mnemonics, designing a poster, making up a short, snappy rhyme or inventing an unusual story that contains key information.

Assessment and GCSE examinations

Schools' Survey

What is your school's policy concerning the assessment of secondary students with dyslexia for GCSE examinations?

Schools rely on SENCOs to use their professional judgement to assess secondary students with dyslexia for GCSE examinations. Additional comments were as follows:

- *'Individual assessment – use of outside agencies, Vernon Spelling, word reading, word chains, free writing (timed), mock examination papers';*
- *'Regarding application for any examination dispensation an educational psychologist's report is required';*

> - 'All students are assessed by the Learning Behaviour Support Team';
> - 'Examination concessions – practice amanuensis etc. so students are familiar with it, help is given with coursework';
> - 'Crib sheets in student's learning medium (pictorial coloured boxes with single words etc.); learning support work with exam officers; educational psychologist to produce appropriate evidence – concessions cleared with parents too.'

Secondary students with dyslexia who are to be considered for special arrangements for their GCSE examinations need to be assessed by an educational psychologist or a suitably qualified teacher (RSA Dip SpLd) two years before examinations take place. Students will be assessed on: reading accuracy, reading speed, spelling, handwriting speed, handwriting legibility and any other specific problems, such as attention and concentration, that may prevent attainment. For diagnostic tests for GCSE and A Level concessions see Chapter 2, Table 2.1 tests marked as ***.

Students with dyslexia are currently allowed 25 per cent additional time in their GCSE and A Level examinations. This is based on GCSE and A Level examinations requiring candidates to write at a rate of 15 words per minute so candidates producing 12 words per minute will need 25 per cent longer to complete each paper. If the candidate's reading age is below 10 for GCSE, or 12 for A Level, based on a single word test, a reader will be required. Completed application forms for special arrangements need to be sent to the awarding bodies.

Schools' Survey

How does your school prepare secondary students with dyslexia for GCSE examinations?

Schools reported that a variety of approaches are used when preparing dyslexic students for GCSE examinations. For example there could be one-to-one-tuition available for students who needed it, or study skills courses, exam practice, question planning, or scrutiny of how exam questions are worded and/or an input from the Learning and Behaviour Support Service.

Booklets offering guidance concerning assessment of GCSE examinations and concessions are available from the examination boards (for addresses see Useful addresses).

PART 2

Enabling secondary students with dyslexia to develop effective study skills

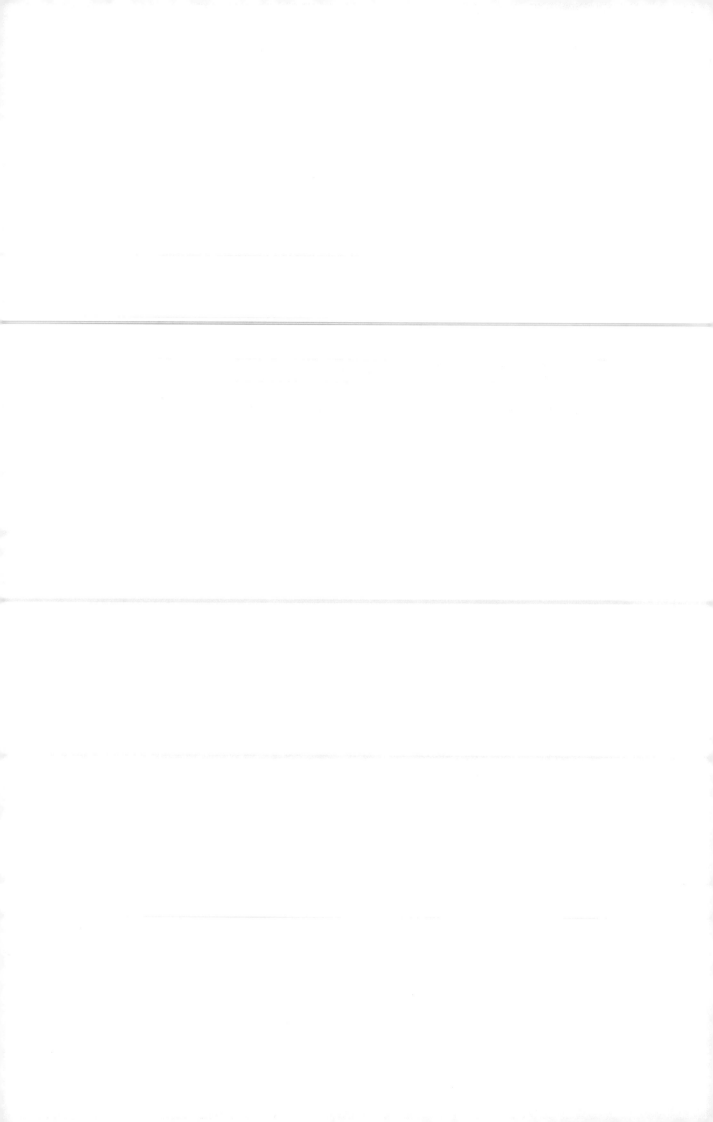

4 Comprehension and study skills

Comprehension is one of the key study skills that secondary students with dyslexia need to develop and master as it is central to successful learning across the curriculum. This chapter addresses the issue of comprehension suggesting that students should be encouraged to think about those subjects, or areas of subjects, that they find hard to understand. Checklists for teachers and LSAs and a worksheet for students are provided so that comprehension can be assessed and strategies, teaching approaches and resources to facilitate understanding are discussed. Particular attention is paid to improving reading comprehension of English at Key Stage 3 (KS3) and Key Stage 4 (KS4).

Identifying difficulties and ways to improve comprehension

Comprehension is the key to successful learning in the secondary school because if students do not understand what they are being taught progress will be limited. It is useful if the student is encouraged to identify those subjects, and in particular what aspects of each subject, they find difficult to understand so that appropriate action can be taken to overcome these problems. A three-stepped model (Figure 4.1) is a useful approach to this.

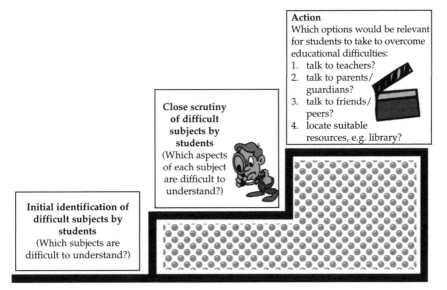

Figure 4.1 A three-stepped model to encourage students to identify and overcome difficulties in understanding specific subjects

---

Schools' Survey

Identify the aspects of each subject which secondary students with dyslexia generally find difficult to understand during their education.

Data from the survey revealed that all coursework could be problematic for dyslexic learners. Schools reported that dyslexic students found the following aspects relating to specific subjects difficult:

English language: *topic words, organising and sequencing information for essay questions, extracting information, writing in detail, spelling/ punctuation and creative writing.*

English Literature: *coping with the volume of reading, understanding texts (particularly Shakespeare), understanding themes and making analogies.*

Maths: *algebra, concepts, number sequencing, symbol recognition and interpreting graphics.*

The sciences: *concepts, relationships, drawing conclusions, subject-specific vocabulary, definitions and calculations.*

History/religious education (RE): *sequencing, concepts, coping with the volume and level of reading, extracting information, interpreting questions to give relevant answers, dates and chronology.*

Geography: *reading maps, extracting information from visual sources and analysing information.*

Students can acquire new knowledge by listening and understanding (listening comprehension) and by reading and understanding (reading comprehension). Periodically staff need to check students' listening comprehension and the following checklist is designed to ensure that lesson objectives are realised.

Checklist to ensure listening comprehension

	Yes	No
1. Can students explain the teaching points in their own words?	☐	☐
2. Can students explain key words in their own words?	☐	☐
3. Can students provide relevant examples to show their understanding of the teaching point(s)?	☐	☐
4. Can students summarise the teaching point(s)?	☐	☐
5. Can students transfer new knowledge to other curriculum subjects? This is important as it demonstrates the practical application and understanding of new concepts.	☐	☐

Reading comprehension is equally as important as listening comprehension. Across the curriculum students will be required to read a text and answer questions on it to demonstrate that they have understood what they have read. Reading comprehension can be assisted by developing oral answers first in preparation for the written responses. The following are useful strategies for subject teachers to prepare students for subsequent written work.

Strategies for developing oral answers in preparation for written work

Before any written work is undertaken:

- Discuss the task as a class.
- Develop oral answers in depth.
- Is there anything which needs to be clarified?
- Write a plan, structure or writing frame on the blackboard/whiteboard to assist students' writing.
- Are the students clear how you would like the work presented?
- Can the students spell key words to be used in the written exercise? Unknown words and meanings will need to be written on the whiteboard/blackboard and in personal dictionaries.
- Have students access to all the information which is required for the written answer?
- Are the students aware of where to find additional information if it is required to complete the task?
- Do any of the students require any special resources in order to complete the written task?
- Would the quality of students' written work be improved if they worked in pairs?

To improve and develop a secondary learner's understanding of lessons across the curriculum it is useful for the SENCO and/or Learning Support Teacher to draw on observations made by subject teachers, LSAs and the student themselves. The following checklists and worksheet are designed to provide this information.

Checklist for subject teachers to assess and improve students' understanding

1. Can the student explain the main point of the lesson in his/her own words?
2. Does the student need to add specialist vocabulary to his/her personal dictionary?
3. Can the student explain specialist words from the lesson in his/her own words?
4. Can the student transfer the knowledge and concepts from your lesson to other curriculum subjects?
5. What resources are needed to develop and reinforce the student's understanding?
6. What teaching strategies and actions need to be taken to improve the student's understanding in subsequent lessons?

The worksheet is to be completed by the student to assess their understanding of a particular lesson. The worksheet can be used in any subject area across the curriculum, but teachers will need to adapt it for specific use by writing key words from their subject on a whiteboard/blackboard.

Many secondary students with special educational needs including those with dyslexia are accompanied by LSAs during lessons. These professionals play a valuable role in assisting student's progress and observations made by the LSA, such as those in the checklist below, offer the subject teacher useful and worthwhile feedback from lessons.

Checklist for Learning Support Assistant's assessment of a student's understanding

Name of student: ....

1. Do you have any information from the student's educational history which could enhance the student's understanding of the lesson?
2. Did the student understand the main point of the lesson?
3. Did he/she have any difficulties following instructions?
4. Does the teacher's language need to be modified so that the student understands the lesson?
5. As a Learning Support Assistant do you need additional resources or do you have to explain key concepts in further detail to facilitate the understanding of your student?
6. Do any of the following affect your student's understanding of the lesson and if so what actions need to be taken to enable academic progress:
    (a) attitude?
    (b) motivation?
    (c) behaviour?
    (d) organisational skills?
7. Does the student understand what he/she has to do for homework?
8. Does the student need additional resources or does the homework have to be rephrased so that it can be completed?
9. Does the student have the appropriate materials and resources for the completion of homework?

Schools' Survey

What teaching methods, strategies and resources are used across the curriculum in your school to facilitate understanding by secondary students with dyslexia?

Schools rely on IEPs, LSA support, Personal, Social and Health Education (PSHE) and homework clubs to facilitate the comprehension of dyslexic students. Frequently, writing frames (a framework provided by the teacher to guide a student's written answer) are used as an additional strategy to promote comprehension in all subjects. Staff training is used to raise awareness about literacy and learning styles. Schools sometimes restrict the GCSE options secondary students with dyslexia can take. It is regular practice within schools for SEN representatives from each department to meet with SENCOs and LSAs to discuss progress of individual students and resources. Worthwhile information arising from these meetings is circulated among school staff.

The data received from schools revealed a variety of approaches are used to facilitate understanding by secondary dyslexic students depending on the subject studied. These are as follows.

English: To facilitate understanding in the English curriculum:

- *reading aloud is encouraged but is not compulsory;*
- *students are given texts without punctuation to stimulate understanding of the use and purpose of punctuation;*
- *Cloze exercises are used to concentrate attention on key words, or use of tense, verbs etc.;*
- *students are asked to paraphrase texts, for example interpret historical texts in modern language;*
- *role play is used to enable students to understand characters in plays and predict events in fiction;*
- *English staff focus on having a positive approach to what students can do rather than what they cannot do;*
- *additional resources are used, e.g. videos, audio tapes, CD-ROMs and films of set books at GCSE and A Level;*
- *from an early age ICT is used to improve written presentation of work;*
- *subject-specific words are highlighted and colour coding is used for folders;*
- *students are encouraged to highlight key words and sentences;*
- *students are taught note-taking skills and drafting procedures.*

Maths: To facilitate understanding in the maths curriculum:

- *students of similar ability are taught together;*
- *small groups often follow the same mathematical curriculum using practical exercises;*
- *the computer program Numbershark is often used (for supplier see Chapter 7);*
- *game cards can be beneficial for mental arithmetic and games can be used to stimulate interest;*
- *where possible attempts are made to relate topics to real life;*
- *maths worksheets use the minimum of words to avoid confusion and to assist comprehension of worksheets staff would offer verbal explanations and boardwork if it was considered necessary.*

Chemistry, physics and biology: To facilitate understanding in the science curriculum:

- *students are taught in small groups and are given extra time and specially adapted SEN resources are used;*
- *laptops are used for recording results;*
- *key words are provided on worksheets as an aid to understanding and spelling;*
- *larger font is used to simplify presentation and text;*
- *text is often read to pupils, e.g. a buddy system is used for reading/ interpretation of material;*
- *information and understanding of concepts is demonstrated by visual aids by teacher and students. Multi-sensory demonstrations are very effective, for example 'hydroelectric power demonstrated through simple rearrangement of pieces of furniture, textbooks to represent harnessing of waterpower'.*

> **The humanities:** To facilitate understanding in the humanities difficult vocabulary is clarified and discussion and questions are used to check comprehension.

Strategies and teaching approaches to develop comprehension across the curriculum

- Assess individual student's level of comprehension with evidence of strengths and areas which need to be developed;
- Consider what skills are required to complete the comprehension task. Are these skills part of the student's repertoire?
- How can the student's strengths be used to complete the comprehension task?
- What strategies and resources are needed to facilitate student's understanding? Select texts and resources to match the interest level of the student and the level of comprehension to be developed and make sure that all professionals are familiar with the resources prior to classroom use;
- To increase comprehension students should be encouraged to:
  1. use their own words rather than quoting from the text;
  2. use different coloured highlighting pens as a useful study aid to identifying different information from the text;
  3. use additional study aids independently – such as: dictionaries, reference books, spellcheckers, technological learning resources (CD-ROMs, DVDs, videos) and study guides etc.;
  4. discuss comprehension difficulties openly;
- Educational visits, related to topics in the curriculum, can be used to enhance comprehension;
- There should be continuous liaison between the SENCO, Learning Support Teacher, subject teachers, LSAs and parents to address the student's comprehension needs.

Comprehension of English at KS3 and KS4

Comprehension plays an prominent role in the KS3 external English examination at and throughout the GCSE syllabus.

Comprehension can be developed before reading takes place. Research conducted by Christen and Murphy (1991) examined the value of using prior knowledge, by considering three possibilities: first by 'building readers' background knowledge', second by 'activating readers' existing background knowledge and attention focussing BEFORE reading' and third by 'guiding readers DURING reading and providing a review AFTER reading'. They argued it may be necessary to take the following action if pupils lack the necessary prior knowledge: teach vocabulary as a prereading step, provide experiences and introduce a conceptual framework which will enable students to build an appropriate background for themselves. They believe prior knowledge is an important step in the learning process, arguing that through building upon previous experiences and connecting them with new ones it is possible to increase students' understanding. This child-centred teaching strategy offers a valuable framework which has meaning for students as it takes into account their personal experiences which can be used as a foundation upon which to build more difficult concepts.

Checklist for reading comprehension at KS3 and KS4

1. **What knowledge and concepts do students need to be aware of prior to reading a text?** For practical purposes identified main themes, ideas, concepts and experiences from the text can be written on the whiteboard/blackboard by teachers. Key points arising from student's personal knowledge can be noted on the board beside each one of these. Once the text has been studied, students' noted knowledge from the board can then be used to compare and contrast with those found in the text.

2. **Use existing experiences and concepts with which the students are familiar and link them with those in the text.** Frequently, the GCSE English language syllabus demands that students analyse newspaper advertisements for GCSE English examinations. In preparation for this analytical exercise students could consider and give reasons for those advertisements which already have had an impact upon them.

3. **Explain difficult concepts in a step-by-step process and give concrete examples that students can relate to.** Students often find Shakespeare difficult to understand at KS3 and KS4. Drama can be used as a vehicle to facilitate the understanding of difficult texts. For example, once students have been given a brief simplified version of the tragedy *Romeo and Juliet*, they could be encouraged to think of similar modern day scenarios which could be dramatised by students in groups. Also videos can be used to enlighten students' understanding of difficult texts.

4. **Encourage students to identify difficult words, phrases and concepts and explain them prior to reading the text.** Students can be encouraged to highlight or underline unknown words, phrases and concepts from individual texts. The teacher can record all of these on the whiteboard/blackboard for class discussion and explanation.

5. **Ask secondary students to give a summary of the text.** Students should always be encouraged to give verbal summaries of texts before written ones are attempted. Good verbal summaries should be modelled on the whiteboard/ blackboard for the benefit of other students.

Comprehension difficulties and secondary students with dyslexia

Literature serves to illustrate the comprehension limitations dyslexic students may encounter throughout their education. Daines *et al.* (1996) highlight the nature of elementary oral comprehension problems. These may include: a misunderstanding of the conditional tense used in instructions, limited vocabulary and the inability to follow instructions without prompting. Other comprehension problems which may arise include inappropriate replies to questions, whereby words alter their meanings in different contexts such as 'sister' (a family relative/a member of a religious order/a senior nurse) and students who take unsuitable literal actions to vernacular phrases such as 'pull your socks up'. Stirling (1985) suggests the adolescent with specific learning difficulties may find figures of speech difficult to understand and may be unable to make deductions from a text. Research indicates how inadequate decoding may cause comprehension problems (Perfetti 1985, Crain and Shankweller 1990, cited in Hulme and Snowling 1994) as can difficulties processing information to obtain meaning and poor metacognitive skills (Paris *et al.* 1983) in pupils with specific learning difficulties. Daines *et al.* (1996), Stirling (1985) and Stothard (1994) outline practical teaching methods which could facilitate pupils' comprehension. These may be used as described or modified by observant practitioners who realise comprehension problems take a wide variety of forms requiring a diverse range of strategies to address individual needs.

Once comprehension difficulties have been identified there is the strong likelihood that new solutions to overcome them will be discovered and delivered. Jones and Charlton (1996) explore this theme of barriers to 'learning' from many perspectives and contexts while simultaneously including theory and legislation, thereby allowing each professional to draw inferences to their specific situation. Adopting a subjective analysis to teaching from this work provides a suitable direction upon which to base future teaching. For example, through employing a multi-sensory approach it is possible to facilitate students' understanding by using CD-ROMs, videos and audio tapes which can be used to reinforce and expand knowledge in areas of difficulty. Liaising with pastoral and academic staff can provide further insights on how to address difficult educational issues which students may be experiencing.

Metacognition means thinking about thinking and it is important to develop the metacognitive ability in secondary students with dyslexia. There are three ways in which this can be developed. Students can be encouraged:

- to verbalise and clarify their thoughts and in doing so written expression can be improved;
- to be self-questioning by asking themselves how and where tasks can be improved. Increasingly students are expected to engage in independent study by completing extended essays and coursework so they need to ask themselves what information would be relevant and where can it be found;
- to find practical ways of overcoming their academic difficulties. For example, for some students in geography rock formation, ox-bow lakes and glaciated hills may pose difficulty. However, by using reference books students can discover what they look like and in due course may be able to photograph their own examples within their neighbourhood (Gough and Tunnmer 1986).

Secondary student's assessment of understanding a lesson

Name:...

1. Explain the main teaching point of the lesson in your own words?

2. Explain how you could link the main teaching point of the lesson with other subjects you are being taught in school?

3. How will you remember what you have learnt from this lesson in the future?

4. Will you need to repeat any part of this lesson again so that you understand it more fully?

5. Can you think of any additional resources which could help you understand the teaching points from this lesson more fully? If so, list them.

5 Day-to-day study skills and secondary students with dyslexia

Improving the day-to-day study skills of students with dyslexia can be the key to unlocking their potential. These study skills include organisation, note-taking, essay writing, reading, revision and exam techniques, and of course memory techniques. This chapter discusses the important role in developing these study skills that is played by partnerships, such as between the student and teacher, the student and their peers and the home–school links. It continues by considering each of the study skills in turn, providing specific information as to how these may be improved.

Schools' Survey

In what way do partnerships within your secondary school contribute to the development of study skills?

Data from the survey indicated that a wide range of in-school partnerships were used to contribute to the development of study skills. The following points were made:

- *In many schools study skills are automatically timetabled as part of the PSHE curriculum.*
- *Some schools have regular interdepartmental meetings to discuss study skills – for GCSEs and A Levels and the preferred learning styles of specific students.*
- *Often schools have training days to address specific aspects of study skills – for example, focusing on 'improving results through improved teaching'.*
- *Often schools appraise all staff to assess the suitability of resources and teaching strategies.*
- *There is the use of shared SEN resources between all departments within schools.*
- *Several schools run after-school clubs or homework clubs in which study skills are taught.*
- *Teachers encourage peer partnerships for cooperative study.*
- *IEPs are employed by staff to develop study skills in specific pupils.*

The role of professional partnerships in developing study skills

Outlined below are the advantages of promoting effective professional partnerships involving good communication in secondary schools.

- A team approach involving out of school multi-professionals (health and education specialists), within school professionals, students and parents offers a holistic perspective to identifying students' study skills needs and achievement.
- Assessment of secondary school students with dyslexia from a multi-professional viewpoint is worthwhile as recurring themes can be prioritised.
- Teams involving multi-professionals can share good models of practice.
- Teams of practitioners may identify skills required by secondary students with dyslexia which are beyond the immediate capabilities of the professionals involved. As a consequence in-service training may need to be organised.
- A team approach to secondary students with dyslexia can advance and clarify the process of identification and assessment, and the development of suitable teaching strategies to improve study skills.

The role of teacher–student partnerships in developing study skills

Successful teacher–student partnerships can enhance study skills in the following ways.

- Teachers have a legal obligation to listen to students and through discussing the demands of the different subjects they study students can offer a valuable insight into their study skills' needs.
- Students can contribute to a study skills programme as they can be actively involved in a teaching or learning strategy.
- By listening to students, practitioners can determine whether students have pastoral, academic or career concerns to be addressed in addition to study skills requirements.

The role of pupil–peer partnerships in developing study skills

Peer partnerships can enhance study skills in the following ways.

- Good models of students' organisational skills, note-taking skills, essay writing, reading skills, revision and examination techniques and memory strategies can be demonstrated and shared with less able students as a vehicle for improvement. More capable students also benefit as they consolidate their learning.

- Seating a secondary student with dyslexia beside a supportive peer in class can often lead to improved work being produced by the less able student while continuing to reinforce knowledge in the supportive peer. Roles can be reversed to ensure equality.
- Encouraging students to swap written work and to discuss how and where it can be developed can lead to a marked improvement in the quality of work.
- Students can assist each other in revision and test each other on information learnt. Furthermore, students should be encouraged to discuss school subjects with peers to discover how the following can be improved throughout the curriculum: note-taking, organisational skills, writing essays, reading, memory strategies, revision and examination techniques.
- It is worthwhile for parents/guardians and students to have the telephone numbers of peers who can be contacted to obtain information regarding forgotten homework.

How home–school partnerships can be effective in developing study skills

There are many advantages of promoting effective home–school partnerships to enhance study skills as parents/guardians and teachers share the same goals in wanting young people in their care to succeed. Parents/guardians can take an active role in encouraging their offspring to discuss all aspects of their school life and by so doing they can offer valuable support in trying to discover ways in which the curriculum can be supplemented out of school hours and being willing to be understanding during periods of revision and exams. In particular parents/guardians can support schools by making sure that their son or daughter:

- is provided with a proper place to study. It is helpful if the room is quiet, warm and well-lit and has bookshelves and a desk for storage of school equipment.
- is properly equipped and organised for lessons and homework. It is *essential* for students to have two sets (one for school and one kept at home) of pens, pencils, sharpeners, coloured crayons, felt tips, rulers, rubbers, compasses, protractors, set squares and a small notebook. The notebook can be used by the student to enter specialised vocabulary and other misspelled words from the curriculum in alphabetical order. In addition, it is *desirable* for students to have a rough notebook, some A4 lined and unlined paper, dictionaries, a spellchecker, Sellotape, Pritt Stick, Tippex, a calculator with spare batteries, plastic wallets for storing notes, files, folders and file dividers for dividing notes into topics and themes.
- has access to a computer and the Internet. Both are sometimes necessary for secondary school assignments. It is the parents'/guardians' responsibility to ensure that the Internet is used correctly.

Parents/guardians should check with the school if any additional equipment is needed for individual subjects in the curriculum.

Home–school partnerships can be forged through parents' evenings, where there is the opportunity to discuss the student's progress formally, and through informal meetings when parents/guardians attend school functions such as sports days and events organised by the school's Parents and Teachers' Association. The partnership can be further strengthened by parents/guardians always keeping the school informed of any circumstances which may affect their son or daughter's education. Sensitive issues such as divorce or bereavement would be treated confidentially and sympathetically.

Throughout secondary education parents/guardians and schools embark on the gradual process of preparing youngsters for further education and leaving school and home. For example supporting the student in their coursework – guiding them as to how to plan and approach their research and how to present it – is useful preparation for further education where often students are expected to submit research assignments. In addition, through encouraging students to take up some of the opportunities provided by schools to travel away from home – sports tours, foreign exchange trips and geography field trips – teachers and parents/guardians can assist in the student's personal development, paving the way for them becoming independent adult citizens. When the student is 16-years-old parents/ guardians and teachers can also provide the student with valuable practical guidance in suggesting and finding a suitable placement for work experience related to their prospective chosen career.

Schools' Survey

What are the practical implications for secondary personnel seeking to improve the study skills of secondary students with dyslexia?

Lack of time was the overwhelming response to the above question. However, how that lack of time was perceived varied between schools, for example:

- *'Time! With all the demands of a full curriculum, there is never enough quality time to devote to this';*
- *'Time in and out of lessons to teach the skills'...;*
- *'Time and resources and the training to do and implement ideas'...;*
- *'Time – too many students and not enough qualified help'...;*
- *'Time – structured schemes of work which jigsaw with subject areas need time to be designed, planned and written and then time to implement.'*

Organisational skills

Organisation plays a crucial role in note-taking, essay writing, effective reading, memory, revision and examination techniques. Secondary students need good organisational skills to follow syllabuses and be successful in exams.

Secondary students will be moving around the school to attend lessons far more than they did in primary school so there is a greater need to be organised. Planning ahead is the key to success, for example by taking three copies of their school timetable and homework timetable – one to be kept in a prominent place at home, such as the kitchen where it is clearly visible, one to be kept where the student studies and the third one to be kept in the student's bag.

Ten timetable tips

1. Examine the timetable for each lesson throughout the curriculum and make a note of the textbooks and equipment which are needed. Record this information on your timetable. You can personalise your timetable either by hand or by computer.

2. At the beginning of lessons get everything you need out ready for the lesson and be prepared to concentrate and work. As soon as the lesson is over make sure you have collected all your belongings.

3. As soon as homework has been given out by a teacher write it down, or copy it from a friend, or obtain it from the teacher at the end of the lesson. Make sure you understand what you need to do for your homework. If you are not quite sure what the teacher expects from you, ask to be shown an example of how it should be completed.

4. Each night prioritise homework. For example, complete the homework which needs to be handed in the next day first and then complete less pressing homework afterwards.

5. Make a note on your timetable of the day when the completed homework needs to be handed in. The hand-in day for each subject could be colour-coded using highlighting pens, making it clearly visible.

6. If you find it difficult to complete your homework approach the teacher first or failing that ask your parents/guardians, or supporting adult or an older student for help.

7. If you are unable to complete the homework for any reason ask your parents/guardians to write a note of explanation to the teacher concerned.

8. Each evening plan and organise what you need for the following day. Think of textbooks, exercise books and sports equipment which are likely to be needed.

9. Try and get yourself into a routine. For every piece of homework you complete reward yourself in some way. Build incentives into your regime, for example complete all your homework before watching a favourite televison programme. On days that you are participating in extra-curricular activities after school try and do some extra study before school in the morning or during your free periods and breaks in the school day.

10. Remember that the whole point of you completing all your homework to the best of your ability is to equip you with skills which will give you greater career options.

The checklist which follows offers guidance about managing time effectively inside and outside school.

Checklist for student to improve organisational skills

Before leaving home check:

- Have you got your pencil case, textbooks, exercise books and homework diary for each of the lessons you have today?
- Have you got all the homework which needs to be handed in today?
- Do you need to bring your sports equipment to school today?

For each lesson:

- Do you know where the next lesson is and what time it starts?
- Do you need a map of the school to find your way around?
- Do you know where to sit in class where you can concentrate without being distracted? Can you see the board easily?
- Do you need to hand in your homework during this lesson?
- Have you made a note of the homework and hand-in date in your homework diary?

Note-taking skills

From the moment students start their secondary education they will be taking lesson notes. Careful thought must be given to their organisation as these form the basis of many essays and will be used for revision and examinations. Many lesson notes taken early on in secondary education will be revisited in greater depth at GCSE and A Level. Note-taking is an active process and can often help students to keep focused during lessons. In addition assignments and essays will require students to make their own notes from reference books.

Ten note-taking strategies
1. What purpose will your notes serve?
2. How are you going to record your notes so that they have meaning for you?
3. Do you have the right equipment to take notes?
4. What will you do with your notes once you have taken them?
5. Would highlighting key words or sentences help you understand your notes or do you need to highlight words in your notes which you do not fully understand to remind you to look up their meaning after the lesson is over?
6. Do you have a system for storing your notes for each subject in the curriculum?
7. Make sure your notes are legible, and leave plenty of space to add additional information later.

---

8. During note-taking look straight at the teacher and listen and concentrate on the teaching points. Listen to the contribution of your contemporaries and make a note of worthwhile comments. If you missed hearing what was being said or did not understand it ask the teacher to repeat or explain it again straight away.
9. Get into the habit of using abbreviations, key words and headings in your notes.
10. Store your notes in an orderly fashion in plastic wallets to protect them as notes need to last a long time and can be used for different purposes throughout your education.

Writing skills

Good essays, assignments and coursework have one quality in common: they are well planned and well organised. Of course, the planning and organisation will depend upon the task which has been set. These guidelines and the checklist that follows could be used by teachers as a class exercise or by students for their personal use.

How to write essays and assignments
1. Obtain and study examples of good essay answers to exam questions from your subject teacher. Note that:
   - the question has been answered using knowledge gained from lessons and from reading textbooks around the subject (information from textbooks is put in the author's own words);
   - if quotations are used to support a point they are short and the source of the quotation is correctly referenced (see Chapter 6);
   - the essay is free from mistakes in spelling, grammar and punctuation.
2. When starting to write your own essays always make sure your essay has a logical structure and that it answers the question. The following techniques offer guidance:
   - Always plan your essays first by brainstorming your ideas/thoughts.
   - Number each thought/idea from your initial brainstorm plan so that they form a logical order. Each point you have thought of should contain a different facet which relates back to the essay title.
   - As you embark on writing your essay or assignment state your ideas clearly in the first sentence of each paragraph. In subsequent sentences support your views with appropriate evidence or information. In the last sentence of each paragraph find a way to sum up your main idea.
3. Make sure you adopt the correct 'tone' for the person who is to mark or judge your work. You will have to find an appropriate writing 'voice' that corresponds to the writing task.

4. Make sure you have answered the essay question.
5. Check that your essay is easy to read and makes sense. You could give it to your parents or friends and ask them how it could be improved, although, this will not be possible for exam/timed essays.
6. Find out if your essay needs to be word processed or handwritten. The advantage of word processing is that the spelling and grammar can be checked. Also, if your teachers wish you to resubmit your work after it has been marked which frequently happens for A Level assignments or modules, it is far easier and quicker to use a computer. However, remember that handwritten practice of timed essays is still essential preparation for external examinations.

Checklist for secondary students in preparation for essay or assignment writing

Place a tick by each completed task.

1. Write down your initial thoughts as to how the question could be answered.
2. Gather together the notes, textbooks, reference books and photocopied material that could be used to help you answer the question.
3. Examine how you could use the selected material to answer the question and organise it into a logical order. It may be helpful to use a highlighting pen to identify key points or themes you could use in your essay.
4. For important essays, assignments or coursework at GCSE and A Level, where your work is going to count towards an examination mark, discuss your views and concerns about how to tackle each piece of work with your subject teacher and tutor. Your contemporaries may have useful suggestions too so be prepared to listen to their suggestions.
5. Write your first draft rephrasing ideas and themes from reference books and text books in your own words to reflect your understanding.
6. Be critical of your first draft by asking yourself how and where could it be improved. Refer to the 'Checklist for students to improve the quality of written work' in Chapter 6 and make any improvements necessary.
7. Write your final version.

In essay and examination questions key words appear that instruct students how the question should be answered. These words need to be understood to avoid disasters. The 'Essay and examination vocabulary worksheet' lists the most commonly used words and can be used by students to find the dictionary definitions. The worksheet can then be used for reference and for testing learned words.

Essay and examination vocabulary worksheet

Name: ....

Word/s	Dictionary definition/your understanding of the term
Account for, account of	
Accurate	
Advantage	
Affect	
Amount	
Approximate	
Analyse	
Carry out	
Cause	
Consider	
Categorise	
Characteristic(s)	
Classify	
Comment	
Compare	
Complete	
Contrast	
Criticise	
Decrease	
Deduce	
Defend	
Define	
Describe	
Diagram	
Disadvantage	
Discuss	
Distinguish	
Drawing	
Effect	
Enumerate	
Essential	
Evaluate	

Essay and examination vocabulary worksheet *cont.*

Word/s	Dictionary definition/your understanding of the term
Example	
Extent	
Explain	
Factor	
Function	
Identical	
Identify	
Include	
Increase	
Information	
Illustrate	
Interpret	
Justify	
Label	
List	
Maximum	
Method	
Minimum	
Necessary	
Outline	
Paraphrase	
Predict	
Process	
Problem	
Purpose	
Prove	
Quality	
Reason	
Relate	
Review	
Sketch	
State	
Summarise	
Synthesise	
Verify	

Having understood the question and spent time planning the essay/ assignment it is important to write a clear and concise introduction to the written work. The following checklist can be used to help with this process.

Checklist for writing introductions to essays

1. Does your introduction explain how the question is going to be answered?
2. Have you included your thoughts or views about the title which could show the knowledge gained from textbooks or lessons in a fresh light?
3. Is there a theme or idea you could mention in your introduction which you could run throughout the essay?
4. Do you need to define any of the terms in the title before responding to the question?

The suggestions given so far apply to all essay and assignment writing but attention is now focused on strategies that can be used for specific types of essay/assignment.

Imaginative and creative essays

Below are some strategies to enable secondary students to produce imaginative and creative essays for English.

Six strategies for writing English essays

1. Write the title of the essay in the middle of the page.
2. Brainstorm the title, that is write down as many ideas which come into your mind as possible. Get into the habit of using and referring to a dictionary. (See p. 82 for an example of a brainstorm, spidergram and mindmap.)
3. Look at your ideas, number all those you could use in your essay in a logical sequence. It is important that your essay is easy to follow.
4. Give some thought to your introduction – for example how are you going to interest the reader? Think about the ending, too. Is it going to be a neat and tidy conclusion or is it going to be dramatic or perhaps end with a question?
5. Try writing a paragraph for each idea or thought you had in your brainstorm. Include your introduction and conclusion.
6. Check your work.

Argumentative essays

An argumentative essay is one that discusses a subject. It is important to be able to organise ideas and link themes clearly.

Checklist for secondary students writing argumentative essays

Check that:

1. there is evidence of systematic and logical thinking;

2. the points are grouped together, and that within each group the points are ordered in a logical sequence with clear connections between them;
3. the evidence, points and ideas are presented objectively;
4. the evidence can withstand close scrutiny;
5. each paragraph flows from the last one. Key words and phrases are used to make the argument/s flow, such as: nevertheless, however, not only...but also, whereas, to illustrate the point we have..., in conclusion, let us compare A with B. Look at how other authors approach this task.
6. The conclusion refers back to the title showing how the question has been answered. It should also offer a solution to the issues, themes or problems raised by the title or exam question.

Descriptive essays

A descriptive essay is one which provides a detailed account of a problem, situation or process.

Checklist for secondary students writing descriptive essays

1. Have you worked out a plan for your essay?
2. Do any of the terms in the title need to be clarified?
3. Can your essay be divided into a number of topics?
4. Too many themes can be confusing in a descriptive essay so can you limit your work to one central theme?
5. Justify your choice of each of the above points in your essay.
6. Your conclusion should:
   (a) pick out and summarise the main points you have described and outline the impact they could have on wider issues;
   (b) offer a solution to the main points you have described;
   (c) show how your essay has answered the question, and how there is a connection between your introduction and conclusion.

Reading skills

In secondary education students will be reading more demanding texts with complex sentence structures. Reading often overlaps and forms the basis of other literacy linked activities such as writing, listening and speaking. The emphasis will be upon using reading skills which have been acquired at primary level to gain new knowledge. In the secondary school, students will need the ability to skim, that is be able to read quickly to obtain the basic information about a subject. Students also need the ability to scan quickly, that is be able to find specific information to be used for assignments, essays and studying.

The curriculum places different reading demands upon secondary students. As a result of this each individual subject teacher has a crucial role to play in developing the student's reading skills in each subject. The following checklist is designed to be used by all subject teachers across the curriculum to enhance the reading skills of secondary students with dyslexia.

Checklist for subject teachers to improve the quality of reading at secondary level

Do you:
1. assess students' reading ability regularly in your subject? Can the student read and understand the textbooks and worksheets you provide in your lessons or does the material need to be adapted? Enlist the SENCO and LSAs to give additional support.
2. make sure that textbooks are at the correct interest and ability level?
3. try and make reading pleasurable and enjoyable in your lessons?
4. always believe students will make progress, albeit in small stages? It is worth noting that belief in students' ability can motivate them to succeed.
5. provide a handout containing references to encourage students to read around your subject? The handout should contain books to correspond with the different reading ability levels in your set or class. A reading list which includes fiction books can also be useful in providing background knowledge and building upon concepts in a stimulating way for your scholars.
6. make sure that students understand abstract concepts they read about in texts and can make practical sense of them?
7. encourage students to give a verbal account of information which has been read? This technique can indicate the level of the student's learning and memory and where it needs to be developed.
8. use different teaching aids to enhance reading and understanding? Some secondary learners respond well to these, for example auditory and visual materials such as: cassettes, CD-ROMs, maps, pictures, graphs and videos.
9. use word tracking exercises to develop students' scanning ability? Word Tracking: High frequency functional words by Betty Lou Kratoville (1993) published by Ann Arbor Publishers provides visual training in left to right directionality, correct spelling, recognition and discrimination skills.
10. use what you know about a student's literacy skills to enhance and extend their reading to a higher and deeper level in your subject? For example, some students already have substantial geographical knowledge which has either been acquired through personal recreational reading, visiting different parts of the world or watching travel programmes. Such a student's geographical interest could be expanded through the provision of teacher-selected fiction and non-fiction books.
11. pick out key themes and words in subject-specific texts and relate it to students' known experiences? Afterwards encourage students to apply knowledge from the text to solve problems. Finally, information from the text can be discussed to discover how it can be applied to a new solution.
12. find different ways of getting students to convey the meaning of a text which has just been read? For example, could the text be dramatised by small groups of students or it could be represented in a visual form?

These days secondary students are encouraged to take an active role in their learning and reading is no exception. Quite often reading in school is linked to a written or verbal activity based upon it. The following checklist and worksheet can be given to secondary students with dyslexia to help them improve their reading skills. It is recommended that teachers discuss the points raised on the checklist with the class.

Checklist for students to improve reading skills

1. Always make sure that you read where there is good light and in a quiet place.
2. Is the size of the print big enough for you? Do you need to wear glasses?
3. Always make sure that you understand what you read. Having access to a dictionary as you read can enable you to look up words you do not understand.
4. Keep a notebook beside you as you read. This can be useful for:
    *   recording words you need to look up later to add to your personal dictionary;
    *   identifying key words which you may need to use when responding to oral or written questions set by your teacher;
    *   recording information as this will focus your mind and will help you to concentrate.
5. Use your school and local library regularly to enhance your academic performance and recreational reading. Perhaps subject teachers could either let you borrow books from them or provide you with a reading list in their subject. Try and build up your own collection of favourite reading material. Get into the habit of browsing and buying your own books from shops. Perhaps you could exchange books with friends. Try and read for a while before you go to sleep. Read around your hobbies and leisure activities and use this information in relevant essays.
6. Be critical of everything you read and get into the habit of discussing and sharing your reading experiences. Remember the more you read the more knowledgeable you will become. You will gain ideas for school work.
7. Increase your reading speed through frequent practice. Read in short bursts if your are finding the material hard. Time your reading and make a chart from which you can record and improve your reading speed. Use the following speed reading checklist to help you in your study.
    *   Which texts can you read quickly in 20 minutes?
    *   Which texts take you a long time to read? (Never read difficult texts when you are tired.)
    *   Time and record yourself reading different texts throughout the curriculum, does a pattern emerge which suggests you need additional support in some subjects? Tell your teacher if you do.
    *   Try and calculate your reading speed. How many words can you read in a minute?

A secondary student's personal reading record

Remember *all* reading is worthwhile. Place a tick in the appropriate column and aim to complete the gaps in your reading.

Name: ....

Type of reading material	I have read	I need to read	Notes on my views of the text with reasons
Adventure fiction			
Auto/biography			
Comics			
Fantasy fiction			
Folk tales			
Historical fiction			
Magazines			
Myths and legends			
Newspapers			
Non-fiction			
Plays			
Poetry			
Romantic fiction			
Science fiction			
Short stories			
Work by other students			
Other reading material			

© Marion Griffiths 2002. *Study Skills and Dyslexia in the Secondary School*. Published by David Fulton Publishers. ISBN: 1 85346 790 1

Revision techniques

The following acrostic poem outlines the key points for term-time revision.

Read all your lesson notes every day,
Every evening write a timed essay,
Very valuable this exercise will be,
It's good to Plan, Organise and Prepare thoroughly,
Set yourself specific targets to improve in your revision,
Each time you work, you're nearer to successful examination.

Six steps for successful revision during term time

1. Believe in yourself. This is the term when all your grades are going to improve.
2. Apply the **POP** approach to your revision – **P**lan, **O**rganise and **P**roduce. If you **p**lan and **o**rganise your work and revision properly, **p**roducing it under examination conditions should be easy.
3. Each night revise a different subject. Read through what you have learnt about the selected subject during the day and write what you can remember about it in 10 minutes, 15 minutes, 20 minutes. This is to prepare you for written examinations. Do not worry if you do not produce much written work at first. Starting early in the term gives you the opportunity to improve your writing speed.
4. Examine your timed written exercise – where do you need to improve your work? Use this knowledge when you approach your written work next time.
5. Do not allow yourself to be distracted during your revision.
6. Find free moments during the school day to do extra revision. Find ways for your fellow students to help you.

Secondary students' self-development action plan for weekly revision (see p. 78)

The idea behind this worksheet is for students to assess and monitor their own revision progress as they proceed through the term. Students need to have several photocopies to correspond with the number of weeks in the term.

Revision timetable for secondary students (see p. 79)

The accompanying timetable is intended for use during term time and holidays. (GCSE and A Level students will be expected to have a revision plan during the holidays as well as during exam leave.)

Secondary student's self-development action plan for weekly revision

Name: ....**Date:** ....

Day/date	Subject revised	What progress did you make? What must you do next time you revise this subject?
Sunday		
Monday		
Tuesday		
Wednesday		
Thursday		
Friday		
Saturday		

REVISION TIMETABLE

(Term-time revision, examination timetable, holiday revision)

NAME ....

	SUNDAY	MONDAY	TUESDAY	WEDNESDAY	THURSDAY	FRIDAY	SATURDAY
MORNING							
AFTERNOON							
EVENING							

© Marion Griffiths 2002. *Study Skills and Dyslexia in the Secondary School*. Published by David Fulton Publishers. ISBN: 1 85346 790 1

Points to remember when planning and organising your revision

- Use your revision timetable to decide which part(s) of the day you can set aside for revision and for each part write in how long you plan to revise.
- Decide the order in which you are going to revise your exams. For example, are you going to revise your weakest subjects first or in the order you are going to sit them?
- Build treats into your timetable – you deserve them. It is very important to take regular breaks. Fresh air and some exercise can be invigorating.
- Spend extra time revising your weaker subjects and if necessary seek help.
- Study old exam papers and think up some questions you could be asked in each subject.
- Keep lists of the topics you have revised at the beginning of each file.
- Get into the habit of summarising topics on portable cards particularly subject matter which may be presenting you with difficulty. Keep these with you so that you can often refer to them.
- Remember each of your subject teachers will be expecting different things from your exam papers and you will need to discover what they are.

Examination techniques

Pressures mount as exam time approaches and it is important for students to remain cheerful and healthy at what can be a stressful period. To achieve this students, parents/guardians and teachers may find the following points to remember useful.

Points to remember during exam time

- Plan treats for when the exams are over such as trips with friends to the cinema/theatre, camping and shopping so there is always something to look forward to afterwards.
- Students need a healthy diet with meals that will give them extra energy, which they will enjoy. Apart from having three well-balanced healthy meals a day, favourite comfort foods can be included to maintain high morale.

Checklist for secondary students preparing for examinations

1. Have you four copies of examination timetables which tell you the day, time and place of the examinations? These copies should be kept in prominent visible places where they will not be missed.

2. Have you the correct equipment for each examination? For example pens, rulers, rubbers, pencils and coloured pencils (sharpened ready for use), a calculator and any specialist equipment such as a protractor for maths.
3. Have you spare equipment to use in exams should you need it? For example, spare pens containing the same coloured ink and spare batteries for your calculator.
4. Are you wearing a watch so you can calculate the time you can spend on each question?

Examination techniques for use during each exam

1. Work out the time limit for each question and write it in pencil beside each question. Keep to the time limits. Always try and write your answer as fully as possible, but should you find yourself short of time use clear bullet points to include information/evidence to illustrate how the question is being answered. Leave some space between each point as you may have time to return to expand each point later.
2. Look at the paper to see how many points are allocated for each question. Always attempt the questions with higher points and the ones you can answer confidently first. Number the questions you are going to answer in order on the paper.
3. Make sure you read and understand each question. Underline key words and always plan your answer before writing it. Everything you write must relate back to the question. Use your knowledge gained from the course to help you. Make sure you write legibly.
4. Always leave a few lines after each question – you might think of something you could add later.
5. Spend 5–10 minutes planning your answer before you write it.
6. Allow 5–10 minutes for checking that your spelling, grammar and punctuation are correct otherwise you may be penalised.

Memory

Secondary students need to develop and enhance their existing memory in order to demonstrate the acquisition of knowledge and learning in examinations.

Memory techniques for secondary students

1. Can you invent a ludicrous story or sentence which involves all the key points which will activate your memory later?
2. Can you invent an acrostic poem or rhyme which contains the vital information?
3. Can you design a poster or spidergram which displays all the knowledge you need?

Figure 5.1 shows a spidergram/mindmap developed by a student to generate ideas in a visual way which can be easily remembered for his essay 'Sunday Dinner'. The point of spidergrams/mindmaps is that only key words or phrases are used and arrows or lines show connections between them. Spidergrams/mindmaps can be used to display the subject matter of curriculum subjects to be revised.

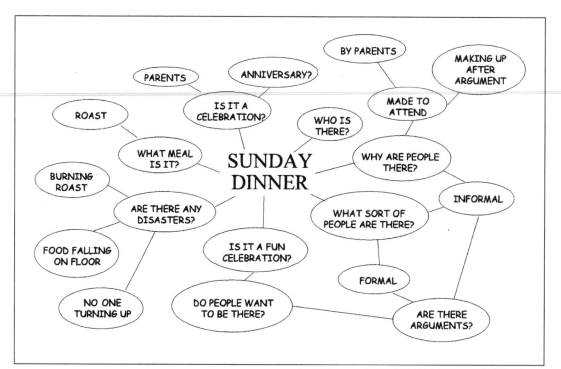

Figure 5.1 Spidergram/mindmap of ideas for an essay called 'Sunday Dinner'

4. Your memory needs to be actively tested in as many different ways possible. Write out key information, say it to yourself, compose a song about it if you are musical, tell your parents and friends what you have just learnt, apply your knowledge to other curriculum subjects and in everyday life. Identify how and where you could improve.
5. Tape key information and replay it to refresh your memory. Key information can be written on small portable cards which can be referred to in the same way.

Schools' Survey

How does your school deliver effective study skills to secondary students with dyslexia?

Schools reported that to develop study skills in dyslexic learners in secondary schools there is much reliance upon one-to-one tuition, the PSHE curriculum and study skills courses. Other schools admitted that study skills teaching was somewhat '*patchy*' within their organisations with assumptions among some staff that study skills should be addressed by the SEN department.

---

6 Developing literacy skills in secondary students

This chapter addresses the issue of developing the literacy skills of secondary students with dyslexia and focuses on spelling, expanding a student's vocabulary and improving the quality of written work. A selection of photocopiable material is provided with explanations of how it can be used. To enhance all aspects of English, students should be encouraged to read widely throughout their secondary education and to assist this suitable texts for different groups are recommended.

Spelling

It is crucial that students are aware how important it is to spell words correctly. For example valuable marks can be lost in GCSE and A level examinations due to poor spelling affecting the overall grade achieved by the student.

Suggestions to improve a student's spelling

1. Ask the student what strategies they use to spell difficult words.
2. Observe the student as they write and spell and note:
   - the words or parts of words which the student spells correctly;
   - the unknown spelling/rule(s) to be acquired.
3. Use existing and understood spelling knowledge to teach unknown words.
4. Encourage the student to examine words closely, noting distinctive letter sequences. Highlighting pens or coloured pencils can be used to draw attention to the complicated part of the word to be learnt. Some students may find it helpful to learn words by breaking them down into syllables.
5. Ask the student to:
   - enunciate the word clearly;
   - visualise the word with their eyes closed, then say and spell it;
   - cover the word and write it saying each letter as it is written;
   - use the learnt word in different sentences.
6. Encourage the student to read and identify spelling mistakes in other students' work. This method of peer editing can improve a student's spelling and critical reading.

Spelling strategies for secondary students

1. Use a small notebook as your personal dictionary to spell new and difficult words.
2. Do not use words you are unable to spell in examinations, think of alternatives.
3. Use a dictionary if you are not sure how to spell words.
4. Make sure you spell words given on examination papers correctly.
5. Make sure you write clearly in exams. Even if you have misspelled the word the examiner can read what you intended to say and you may not be penalised, whereas, an illegible word could lose you marks.

Regular practice at spelling commonly misspelled words can improve a student's spelling. The two 'Spelling practice' worksheets are provided for this purpose. The first of these worksheets is a sample worksheet and the other is a blank master that can be copied and different sentences inserted (a list of suitable sentences is given on pp. 87 and 88).

Expanding a student's vocabulary

The greater a student's vocabulary the easier it is for them to use their own words to answer questions and write essays or assignments.

The worksheet 'Understanding words' is designed to increase the student's vocabulary and comprehension of words. Two copies of this worksheet are provided, a sample copy and a blank master that can be photocopied and different groups of words inserted (a list of suitable words and their definitions is given on pp. 89–94). The teacher needs to explain to the student the different stages of the worksheet and how they are to be completed. For example:

1. Draw attention to the word endings of each sheet and the sound which is made. For example, the ending *ion* as in act*ion* makes the sound 'shun', the word ending *ious* as in ted*ious* makes the sound 'hus' and the word ending *our* as in the word flav*our* makes the sound 'or'.
2. Before the student copies the word underneath on the dotted line encourage them to read and offer the meaning of the word.
3. The student then needs to look up the dictionary definition and write it in the box.
4. To demonstrate that the student has understood the word they then have to use it in a sentence of their own.

Spelling practice

Rewrite the sentences below on the lines provided to include the correct spelling from the brackets.

1. The pupils prepared to (revise, rivise) (their, there, they're) school subjects during the Easter holidays.

....

....

....

....

2. The family (exspeketed, expected) to go to (Florida, Florider) for their summer holidays.

....

....

....

....

3. During the second world war innocent people were (tortured, torturod) in (consantration, concentration) camps.

....

....

....

....

4. The actors (screemed, screamed) (incredibly, increadably) realistically for the audience

....

....

....

....

Spelling practice

Rewrite the sentences below on the lines provided to include the correct spelling from the brackets.

1.

....

....

....

....

2.

....

....

....

....

3.

....

....

....

....

4.

....

....

....

....

Sentences for use in 'Spelling practice' worksheets

1. The (plesant, pleasant) and (cheerful, cheerfull) dressmaker (spred, spread) her sewing on the (table, tabul) to work.
2. It was time to catch the (plain, plane) to (Heathrow, Heethrow) airport.
3. Charities such as The British Red Cross aim to help (refugles, refugees) in different parts of the (world, werld).
4. In the traffic jam the car remained (stationery, stationary) as there was a (multipal, multiple) pile-up ahead.

1. The wedding guests (went, whent) to a lavish reception at the hotel.
2. As it was wet outside the farmer could not decide (weather, whether) to (wear, where) a coat for his ramble.
3. Often the (doctor, docter) was used to dealing with difficult (patience, patients) in her surgery.
4. A (friend, freind) of my mother's lives in a (wonderful, wonderfull) house.

1. The patient wrote to his friend explaining that he was (feeling, fealing) a (great, grate) deal (beter, better).
2. Every (Saterday, Saturday) the old man bought (sanwiches, sandwiches) crisps and (drincks, drinks) from the local supermarket.
3. Many (passngers, passengers) have difficulty travelling on (trans, trains) with (heavy, hevy) cases, often gangways are (paked, packed) full.
4. The menu was brought to the hotel guests by the (inexperienced, inexpurienct) waiter.

1. The television (documentury, documentary) (feetured, featured) many aspects of (wild, wilde) life.
2. The (pieces, peaces) of a jigsaw can be (independently, independantly) put together.
3. As the diver submerged into the (see, sea) he realised that this (would, wood) be a most exciting experience.
4. The newspaper contained (many, meny) interesting (articles, articals).

1. Following the Dunblane disaster public opinion demanded (tighter, tightor) control (of, off) gun laws.
2. Many (travelers, travellers) consider using the Eurotunnel as a (convenient, conveniant) (way, weigh) of going to France.
3. The actress attended the glittering awards (ceremony, ceremone), however she had difficulty (rembering, remembering) her acceptance speech.
4. It was a (purfect, perfect) day for going for a walk.

1. From the coach spectacular views of the (contryside, countryside) could be (scene, seen).
2. The children used their (personnel, personal) stereos to listen to their favourite (music, musique).

3. In the (sumer, summer) the following sports prove (poplar, popular), namely (tennis, tenis), (crikket, cricket) and (swiming, swimming).
4. The model was very difficult to make and Sharon had to read the (intrutshuns, instructions) carefully.

1. January is the month which marks the (beging, beginning) of the year.
2. The old lady would have preferred fresh (bred, bread) for her breakfast.
3. During the night gale force winds broke the garden (fens, fence).
4. Four essential (ingredients, ingrediants) are needed to make a pizza base: flour, yeast, margarine and water.

1. One hot sunny day the (feasant, pheasant) walked around the edge of the (flour, flower) bed.
2. The (stroke's, stroak's) instruction for a spurt enabled the rowing eight to win the race by five lengths.
3. It was a moment of great honour (for, four) the celebrity to be (presented, presentet) to the Queen.
4. 'Make the most of your opportunities' the teacher (advised, adviced) her pupils.

1. The American (kernal, colonel) was an outstanding raconteur.
2. (Aminals, Animals) should be kept in their natural habitat, declared the vet.
3. Many bargain-hunters look forward to the summer (sales, sails).
4. (Houseman, Housman) was a famous poet who went (to, two) Bromsgrove School.

1. 'It isn't (fair, fayre)' the pupil protested, 'it is (not, knot) my (mistake, misteak).'
2. The students had to (weight, wait) a long time for the bus to arrive.
3. 'Keep in (thyme, time) with me' the (conducter, conductor) told the (orchestra, orchestrer).
4. The (cleaner, kleener) admitted he had accidentally broken an (ornament, ornameant).

1. The (principle, principal) of the university gave an (excellent, excellant) speech.
2. Ashwin (knows, nose) he has to be well-behaved to be (aloud, allowed) to go on holiday with his school friend.
3. Life is full of (suprises, surprises).
4. Security guards were on the look-out for violence at the (statshun, station).

1. The teacher stood (by, bye) the wall on playground duty.
2. 'We wish you would stay at (our, are) house a little longer,' the hosts said to their visitors.
3. The (fone, phone) rang loudly and the (gril, girl) rushed to answer it.
4. 'It's (bean, been) a long time since I last went (swimming, swiming)' (siad, said) the teenager.

© Marion Griffiths 2002. *Study Skills and Dyslexia in the Secondary School*. Published by David Fulton Publishers. ISBN: 1 85346 790 1

Understanding words

Copy the words underneath on the lines provided.

station   election   action   function

_____ ‾ _____ ‾ _____   _____ ‾

Write the dictionary definition of each word using the boxes provided.

Insert the words in brackets to make sentences of your own using the lines provided.

1. (station) ....

....

....

2. (election) ....

....

....

3. (action) ....

....

....

4. (function) ....

....

....

Understanding words

Copy the words underneath on the lines provided.

_____ -   _____ -   _____   _____ -

Write the dictionary definition of each word using the boxes provided.

Insert the words in brackets to make sentences of your own using the lines provided.

1. (   )...
....
....

2. (   )...
....
....

3. (   )...
....
....

4. (   )...
....
....

Words for use in 'Understanding words' worksheet (with definitions)

station – Station is a place where passenger trains stop on a railway line, typically with platforms and buildings.

election – Election is formal and organised choice by vote of a person for a political office or other position.

action – Action is the fact or process of doing something, typically to achieve an aim.

function – Function is an activity or purpose intended for a person or thing.

generation – Generation describes all the people born and living at about the same time, regarded collectively.

fraction – A fraction is a numerical quantity that is not a whole number.

relation – A relation is the way in which two or more concepts, objects or people are connected.

devotion – Devotion means love, loyalty or enthusiasm for a person, activity or cause.

mention – Mention means to refer to something briefly without going into detail.

suction – Suction means the production of a partial vacuum by the removal of air in order to force fluid into a vacant space or procure adhesion.

nation – Nation means a large aggregate of people united by common descent, history, culture or language inhabiting a particular state or territory.

section – Section means any of the more or less distinct parts into which something is or may be divided or from which it is made up.

deception – Deception is the action of deceiving someone.

notion – Notion is a conception or belief about something.

tuition – Tuition is the teaching or instruction especially of individuals pupils or small groups.

attention – Attention means the notice taken of someone or something.

addition – Addition is the action or process of adding or joining something to something else.

preparation – Preparation is the action or process of making ready for use or consideration.

option – Option means a thing that is or may be chosen.

reception – Reception is the action or process of receiving something sent, given or inflicted.

sensation – Sensation is a physical feeling or perception resulting from something that happens or comes into contact with the body.

competition – Competition is the activity or condition of striving to gain or win something by defeating or establishing superiority over others engaged in the same attempt.

© Marion Griffiths 2002. *Study Skills and Dyslexia in the Secondary School*. Published by David Fulton Publishers. ISBN: 1 85346 790 1

separation – Separation is the action or state of moving or being moved apart.

ventilation – Ventilation is the provision of air to a room or building and so on.

direction – Direction is the course along which someone or something moves.

circulation – Circulation is the movement to and fro or around something especially that of fluid in a closed system.

consideration – Consideration means careful thought typically over a period of time.

prescription – A prescription is an instruction written by a medical practitioner that authorises a patient to be issued with medicine or treatment.

position – Position means a place where someone or something is located or has been put.

traction – Traction is the action of drawing or pulling a thing over the surface, especially over a road or track.

perfection – Perfection is the condition, state or quality of being free or as free as possible from all flaws or defects.

invasion – An invasion is for instance where a country is invaded by an armed force.

conversation – Conversation is talk especially an informal one between two or more people in which news or ideas are exchanged.

inspection – Inspection is the action or process of looking at or someone or something closely, typically to assess their condition or to discover any shortcomings.

ambition – Ambition is a strong desire to do or achieve something, typically requiring determination and hard work.

exclamation – Exclamation is a sudden cry or remark especially expressing surprise.

decoration – Decoration is the process or art of decorating or adorning something.

exhibition – Exhibition is a public display of works of art or other items of interest held in an art gallery, an art museum or at a trade fair.

formation – Formation is the action or process of being formed. It can also mean a structure or arrangement.

information – Information means facts provided or learned about something or someone.

motion – Motion is the action or process of moving or being moved.

friction – Friction is the resistance that one surface or object encounters when moving over another.

preposition – Preposition is a word governing and usually preceding a noun or pronoun and expressing a relation to another word or element in the clause.

population – Population is the word given to all the inhabitants of a particular town, area or country.

examination – Examination is detailed inspection or investigation.

destruction – Destruction is the action or process of causing so much damage to something that it no longer exists or cannot be repaired.

creation – Creation is the action or process of bringing something into existence.

subscription – Subscription is the action of making or agreeing to make an advance payment in order to receive or participate in something or as a donation.

composition – Composition is the nature of something's ingredients or constituents, that is the whole way in which something is made up.

protection – Protection is the action of protecting someone or something. It is usually a person or thing that prevents someone or something from suffering harm or injury.

question – Question is a sentence worded or expressed so as to elicit information.

indigestion – Indigestion is pain or discomfort in the stomach associated with difficulty in digesting food.

pension – A pension is a regular payment made by the state to people of or above the official retirement age and to some widows and disabled people.

tension – Tension is the state of being stretched tight.

mansion – Mansion is a large impressive home.

cushion – A cushion is a bag of cloth stuffed with a mass of soft material, used as a comfortable support for sitting or leaning on.

odour – Odour is a distinctive smell, frequently an unpleasant one.

flavour – Flavour is the distinctive quality of a particular food or drink as perceived by the taste buds.

parlour – Parlour is a dated word used to describe a sitting room in a private house.

vapour – Vapour is substance diffused or suspended in the air, especially one normally liquid or solid.

vigour – Vigour means physical strength and good health.

saviour – A saviour is a person who saves someone or something especially a country or cause from danger and who is regarded with the veneration of a religious figure.

labour – Labour is work which is usually hard and physical.

glamour – Glamour is the attractive or exciting quality which makes certain people or things seem appealing or special.

harbour – A harbour is a place on the coast where ships may moor in shelter.

rumour – A rumour is a story or report which is currently circulating of doubtful or uncertain truth.

colour – Colour is the property possessed by an object of producing different sensations on the eye as a result of the way it reflects or emits light.

favour – Favour is an attitude of approval or liking.

honour – An honour is a mark of great respect or high public regard that is a privilege to be given or received.

armour – Armour describes the metal coverings formerly worn by soldiers or warriors to protect the body in battle.

humour – Humour is the quality of being comic, especially as expressed in literature or speech.

behaviour – Behaviour is the way in which one acts or conducts oneself.

unique – Unique is an adjective which is used to mean one of its kind, unlike anything else.

antique – An antique is a collectable object having high value because of considerable age.

oblique – Oblique means slanting. It is neither parallel nor at right angles to a specified or implied line.

cheque – A cheque is an order to a bank to pay a stated sum from the drawer's account, written on a special form.

picturesque – Picturesque is an adjective that describes something which is visually attractive, especially in a quaint or pretty style.

technique – Technique is the way of carrying out a particular task, especially the execution or performance of an artistic work or scientific procedure.

grotesque – Grotesque means comically or repulsively ugly.

discotheque – A discotheque is a club or party at which people dance to pop music.

connection – Connection is a relationship in which a person, thing or idea is linked with something else.

protection – Protection is a person or thing that prevents someone or something from suffering harm or injury.

education – Education is the process of receiving or giving systematic instruction, especially at school or at university.

pretension – Pretension is a claim, aspiration or assertion of a claim to a certain status or quality.

completion – Completion is the action or process of finishing something.

expansion – Expansion is the action of becoming larger or more extensive.

action – Action is the fact or process of doing something, typically to achieve an aim.

propulsion – Propulsion is the action of driving or pushing forward.

communication – Communication is the imparting or exchanging of information by speaking, writing or by using some other medium.

resolution – A resolution is a firm decision to do or not to do something.

delegation – A delegation is a body of delegates or representatives.

omission – An omission is someone or something that has been left out or excluded.

confusion – Confusion means that there is uncertainty about what is happening, intended or required.

description – A description is a spoken or written representation or account of a person, object or event.

attention – Attention means the notice taken of someone or something: the regarding of someone or something as interesting or important.

extension – Extension is a part that is added to something to enlarge or prolong it.

infusion – Infusion is a drink, remedy or extract prepared by soaking the leaves of a plant or herb in liquid.

suspicion – Suspicion is a feeling or thought that anything is possible, likely or true.

delusion – A delusion is an idiosyncratic belief or impression which is firmly maintained despite being contradicted by what is generally accepted as reality or rational argument; typically a mental disorder.

expulsion – Expulsion is the action of depriving someone of membership of an organisation.

provision – Provision is the action of providing or supplying something of use.

confession – Confession is a formal statement admitting that one is guilty of a crime.

revision – Revision is the action of revising.

conversions – Conversion is the process or action of changing or causing something to change from one form to another.

desperation – Desperation is an act of despair, typically one which results in rash or extreme behaviour.

adulation – Adulation is excessive admiration or praise.

trepidation – Trepidation is a feeling of fear or agitation about something that may happen.

reconciliation – Reconciliation is an act or process of causing someone or something to work in harmony. It can also mean to make or show someone or something to be compatible.

distinction – Distinction means the difference or contrast between similar things or people.

division – Division is the action of separating something into parts, or the process of being separated.

diversion – Diversion is an instance from turning something aside from its course.

distraction – Distraction is a thing that prevents someone from giving their full attention to something else.

correction – Correction is the action or process of correcting or rectifying something.

mediation – Mediation is the process of intervening between people in a dispute in order to bring about an agreement or reconciliation.

extradition – Extradition is the action of handing over a person accused or convicted of a crime to the jurisdiction of the foreign state in which the crime was committed.

nomination – Nomination is the action of nominating or state of being nominated, that is, to formally propose a candidate for election for an honour or an award.

evaporation – Evaporation is the process or action which turns liquid into vapour.

violation – Violation is the act of violating something, that is failing to comply with a rule or formal agreement.

indention – Indention is the act of indenting, positioning a text further in from the margin than the main part of the text.

isolation – Isolation is the process or fact of isolating or being isolated, that is, being away from other places, buildings or people.

famous – Famous means known by many people.

dangerous – Dangerous means something, or someone that is likely to cause injury or harm.

tremendous – Tremendous means very great in amount, scale or intensity.

numerous – Numerous means many or great in number.

anxious – Anxious means experiencing worry, nervousness or unease, typically about an imminent event or something with an uncertain outcome.

furious – Furious means extremely angry.

mysterious – Mysterious means that it is something which is difficult or impossible to explain or understand.

suspicious – Suspicious means showing cautious distrust of someone or something.

© Marion Griffiths 2002. *Study Skills and Dyslexia in the Secondary School*. Published by David Fulton Publishers. ISBN: 1 85346 790 1

Improving the quality of a student's written work

Students need to be able to express themselves in writing so that is is clear what they are trying to say and to this end they should be encouraged to become self-critical of their written work, checking that it makes sense, that points are made in a logical order and that it is as free from as many spelling, punctuation and grammatical errors as possible. The following checklist is aimed at improving the written work of secondary students with dyslexia.

Checklist for students to improve the quality of written work

Before handing in any written work, check it thoroughly for the listed points.

1. Does your work ANSWER the question?
2. Is your written work STRUCTURED? Does your work have a FRAMEWORK? Have you used paragraphs correctly?
3. Have you checked your written work:
   - for SPELLING?
   - for the correct use of PUNCTUATION?
   - for GRAMMATICAL ERRORS?
   - to see that you have avoided the REPETITION of words and phrases?
4. Have you provided sufficient EVIDENCE and DETAIL in your answer?
5. Have you used the correct referencing convention when QUOTING from the text to support your answer? Here is an example from a student's essay about Romeo and Juliet. Note that the quotation is only a few words so there is no need to start a new line:

   > *Notice through the Chorus's speech at the beginning of Romeo and Juliet we are told the ending of the play, 'their death-marked love.' (L.9).*

   However, if your quote is more than a few words you will need to begin your quote on a new line remembering to use quotation marks. Here is an example:

   > *Capulet tells Paris his daughter is not yet fourteen years old:*
   > *'My child is yet a stranger in the world;*
   > *She hath not yet seen the change of fourteen years.' (11. 8-9)*

6. Have you missed out any words in your sentences? It may help you to read your work out loud.
7. Have you written what you MEANT to say? Have you expressed yourself CLEARLY?
8. AVOID using words such as doesn't, weren't. If you need to use them write them out in FULL.
9. Have you COPIED words correctly from the text and the board?
10. Is your writing LEGIBLE?

Secondary students will be called upon to read, discuss, analyse and write about different types of texts throughout the curriculum. The following guide is designed to assist this process by posing questions which can be answered by the student through close reading of the text. A student may be required to write a review of a book that they have read. The 'Book review worksheet' provides the student with a framework for tackling this task.

Book review worksheet

Book review by _____

Title of book_____

Author of book _____

INTRODUCTORY PARAGRAPH (Begin by stating the full title and the author's name, you may include biographical information about the author.)

SECOND PARAGRAPH (Give a brief outline of the story. Describe the way in which the story develops, mentioning key events. Describe a favourite incident giving reasons why you have chosen it.)

THIRD PARAGRAPH (You should consider the contribution of the characters to the plot. Say how their personalities change throughout the novel. Are the characters true to life and has the author created convincing people?)

FOURTH PARAGRAPH (Consider the way the book has been written and also consider the themes and issues. Is it suitable for boys and girls? Are there unexpected twists in the story? Or can you tell what is going to happen next? Is the story fast moving and exciting?)

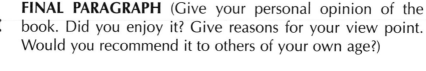

FINAL PARAGRAPH (Give your personal opinion of the book. Did you enjoy it? Give reasons for your view point. Would you recommend it to others of your own age?)

© Marion Griffiths 2002. *Study Skills and Dyslexia in the Secondary School*. Published by David Fulton Publishers. ISBN: 1 85346 790 1

A guide to reading texts for secondary students

1. Who is telling this story or giving this account? Is the author addressing you directly or is it written in the first person or third person? Perhaps the writer has used a character to speak to the reader.
2. Who is being spoken to in the text? Is it the general public, a particular person or is the writer in a reflective mood and speaking to themselves?
3. Do you know the origins of the text? How does this knowledge add to your understanding or interpretation of it?
4. How would you categorise this text? Does it have a recognisable form?
5. What does the writer expect from you after reading the text? Do they expect you to share the same opinions or be persuaded to do something?
6. What is your opinion of the text? For example, what are your views concerning the author's choice of content, the way in which characters are depicted, the descriptive vocabulary, dialogue, themes or setting?

Schools' Survey

What methods, strategies and resources are used in your school to develop literacy skills throughout the curriculum for secondary students with dyslexia?

The following in-school and in-class approaches were used by schools to enhance literacy skills.

- *There was close scrutiny of students' progress, particularly in reading.*
- *A computer system entitled SuccessMaker (for more information see Chapter 7) was used to increase students' numeracy and literacy skills and the use of laptops in all subject areas.*
- *Key word lists were given in individual subjects.*
- *Students were given hand-held spellcheckers to use.*
- *Writing frames (a framework provided by the teacher to guide a student's written answer) were given by teachers;*
- *'Fast Forward' (see Chapter 7) was given to Year 7 pupils. This is a complete study skills resource based on a range of articles to develop listening, organisation, note-taking, writing reports and summaries.*
- *Many schools employed reading recovery programmes.*
- *Students have access to individual specialist teaching.*
- *Differentiated texts were used.*
- *Specific resources such as Wordshark 2L, Word Bar and* Alpha to Omega *were used. (These resources are explained in Chapter 7.)*

Recommended reading for different age groups

Many of the books listed here will be available in school or local libraries. Fiction books such as these will usually be shelved alphabetically under the author's last name.

Age group 11–14 years

Author	Title	Author	Title
Burgess, M.	*Cry of the Wolf*	Kipling, R.	*Stalky and Co*
Carroll, A.	*Rosie's Quest*	Lewis, C. S.	*The Lion, the Witch and the Wardrobe*
Cruise, B.	*Going, Going, Gone*		
Durrell, G.	*My Family and Other Animals*	O'Hara, E.	*The Hiring Fair*
		Palmer, M.	*Sagittarius – Missing*
Fine, A.	*Goggle-eyes*	Pullman, P.	*The Tin Princess*
Hodgson Burnett, F.	*The Secret Garden*	Tomlinson, T.	*The Rope Carrier*
		Warburton, N.	*To Trust a Soldier*
Howarth, L.	*Maphead*	Westall, R.	*The Machine Gunners*
Hoy, L.	*United on Vacation*		

Age group 14–16 years

Author	Title	Author	Title
Adams, R.	*Watership Down*	Melville, P.	*The Ventriloquist's Tale*
Banks, L. R.	*Maura's Angel; Broken Bridge; The Mystery of the Cupboard*	Moore, B.	*The Magician's Wife*
		O'Brien, E.	*House of Splendid Isolation; Down by the River*
Blume, J.	*Here's to you, Rachel Robinson; Tiger Eyes*	Prince, M.	*Memoirs of a Dangerous Alien*
Cross, G.	*New World*		
Dahl, R.	*Ah, Sweet Mystery of Life*	Rice, A.	*Interview with the Vampire; The Vampire Lestat; Queen of the Damned*
Davis, J.	*If Only I'd Known*		
Fine, A.	*Step by Wicked Step*		
Foreman, M.	*Warboy*	Salinger, J. D.	*Catcher in the Rye; Franny and Zooey*
Gleitzman, M.	*Misery Guts*		
Hardcastle, M.	*Please Come Home*	Sallis, S.	*No Time At All*
Hemingway, E.	*The Old Man and the Sea*	Sillitoe, A.	*The Loneliness of the Long Distance Runner*
Herriot, J.	*All Creatures Great and Small*	Tolkien, J. R. R.	*The Hobbit; The Lord of the Rings*
Howarth, L.	*Weather Eye*	Townsend, S.	*The Queen and I*
Hughes, T.	*The Iron Woman*	Wall, A.	*The Eden Mission*
Jennings, P.	*Thirteen! Unpredictable Tales*	Waugh, S.	*The Menyals*

Age group 16–18 years

Author	Title	Author	Title
Adams, D.	*The Long Dark Tea-time of the Soul*	De Bernières, L.	*Captain Corelli's Mandolin*
Bainbridge, B.	*An Awfully Big Adventure*	Fitzgerald, F. Scott	*The Great Gatsby*
Braithwaite, E. R.	*To Sir, With Love*	Gaardner, J.	*Sophie's World*
Christie, A.	*And Then There Were None*	Gibbons, S.	*Cold Comfort Farm*
		Golding, W.	*Lord of the Flies*

Age group 16–18 years *cont.*

Author	Title	Author	Title
Huxley, A.	*Brave New World*	Twain, M.	*Adventures of Huckleberry Finn*
Lee, H.	*To Kill a Mockingbird*		
Orwell, G.	*Animal Farm; Nineteen Eighty-four*	Verne, J.	*Around the World in Eighty Days*
Pratchett, T.	*Good Omens*	Wyndham, J.	*The Day of the Triffids*
Townsend, S.	*The Secret Diary of Adrian Mole aged 13³/₄*		

Reading schemes for secondary students who are reluctant readers

High Impact (4 secondary age ranges)
This reading scheme is published by Heinemann Educational.
Contact information: Heinemann Educational, Customer Services, Reed Publishers, Linacre House, Jordan Hill, Oxford OX2 8EJ; www.heinemann.co.uk

Spirals (for older readers)
This reading scheme is published by Stanley Thornes.
Contact information: Stanley Thornes, Ellenborough House, Wellington Street, Cheltenham, Glos. GL50 2YD.

7 Resources to develop study skills

There are a wide variety of resources available to assist practitioners in the development of study skills for students with dyslexia. This chapter provides details of books, equipment, computer programs and packages, videos and accompanying books and reading schemes that have been found to be useful. All the information was correct at the time of publication.

Schools' Survey

List the books, CD-ROMs, audio cassette tapes and other resources your school finds useful when developing study skills in secondary learners with dyslexia.

Schools found the following resources useful to develop study skills:

writing frames, Inspirations CD-ROM, Clicker 4, Starspell, Encarta, Eye 4 Spell, touch-typing programmes, BBC Bitesize videos, revision guides, Powerpoint, Excel and the Internet.

Books to develop literacy skills

Cripps, C. (1986) *Catchwords Ideas for Teaching Spelling*. London: Harcourt Brace.

Crystal, D. (1988) *Rediscover Grammar*. London: Longman.

Daughtrey, S. J. (1995) *Grammar*. Buckinghamshire: Child's World Education.

Daughtrey, S. J. (1995) *Punctuation*. Buckinghamshire: Child's World Education.

Daughtrey, S. J. (1995) *Spelling Rules and Practice*. Buckinghamshire: Child's World Education.

Dunsbee, T. and Ford, T. (1980) *Mark My Words*. London: Ward Lock.

Hornsby, B. and Shear, F. (1999) *Alpha to Omega*, 5th edn. London: Heinemann Educational. A structured spelling programme suitable for ages 5–adult.

Moseley, D. (ed.) (1995) *ACE Spelling Dictionary*, 7th edn. Wisbech, Cambs: LDA. Suitable for ages 7–adult to find words using initial vowel sound and initial sound. Available from good book shops.

Stirling, E. G. (1993) *Help for the Dyslexic Adolescent*, 8th edn. Sheffield: St. David's College.

Sutton, C. (1981) *Communicating in the Classroom*. London: Hodder & Stoughton.

Useful equipment for secondary learners with dyslexia

Cerium Overlays are useful for students who find it beneficial to have a coloured overlay when reading a text. *Contact information:* Cerium Technology, Appledore Park, Appledore Road, Tenterden, Kent TN30 7DE. Email: ceriumngrp@aol.com; website: www.ceriumvistech.co.uk.

Listening books from The National Listening Library suitable for all ages including GCSE course books. Further information is available from Lisa Knightsbridge. *Contact information:* Lisa Knightsbridge, 12 Lant Street, London SE1 1QH. Tel: 020 7407 9417; email: lknightsbridge@listening-books.org.uk; Website: www.listening-books.org.uk

Quicktionary is a reading pen which displays syllables, spells the word out loud, keeps a history of scanned words, scans inverted and hyphenated text, contains over 200,000 dictionary definitions, and is adjustable for left- and right-handed users. *Contact information:* Available from iANSYST Ltd, The White House, 72 Fen Road, Cambridge CB4 IUN. Tel: 01223 420101; FAX: 01223 426644.

Visual Tracking Magnifier is an optical device which is a high powered magnifying glass with a central viewing strip. It sits on the page and can be easily tracked backwards and forwards across the text. *Contact information* Edward Marcus Ltd, Tel: 01298 871388; FAX: 01298 871064.

Information computer technology

AVP produces a comprehensive selection of software to meet all the curriculum needs in the secondary school (11–adult). *Contact information:* Tel: 01291 625439; FAX: 01291 6622671

Computer Users Bulletin published by the Computer Resources Group of the British Dyslexia Association is a good source of information about suitable programs and packages. *Contact information:* British Dyslexia Association (BDA), 98 London Road, Reading RG1 5AU. Tel: 0118 966 2677.

EndNote is a software package that can be used as:

- an on line search tool – it provides a simple way to search on line bibliographic databases and retrieve the references into EndNote. It can also import data files saved from a variety of on line services, CD-ROMs and library databases.

- a reference database – it specialises is storing, managing, and searching for bibliographic references in your private reference library.
- a bibliography maker – it builds lists of cited works automatically. Use EndNote to insert citations into word processing documents and later scan those documents for in-text citations to compile a bibliography in any format you need.

Contact information United Kingdom/Ireland: Adept Scientific plc, Amor Way, Letchworth, Herts. SG6 1ZAA UK. Tel: 01462 480055; FAX: 01462 480213; email: info@adeptscience.co.uk; Website: www.adeptscience.com

Contact information USA: ISI ResearchSoft, 800 Jones Street, Berkeley, CA 94710 USA. Tel: (510) 559–5982 (country code is 001); FAX: (510) 5598–8683 (country code is 001); email: pc-endnote@issiresearchsoft.com (technical support); info@issiresearchsoft.com (customer service) Website: www.endnote.com

Hi-Spell Computer Software provides material suitable for ages 5–16 and contains 3 suites of 5 programs each (19 disks in total). The programs cover many language topics, including keyboard skills and grammatical construction of a sentence. *Contact information:* Hi-Spell Computer Software, 114 Rainhill Road, Merseyside L35 4PH. Tel: 01514 269988.

iANSYST Ltd produce a variety of dictation systems, software packages to make your computer speak, dictionaries, encyclopedias and reading and writing programs to enable students with dyslexia make the most of their abilities. An example is Wordswork, a multi-sensory approach to teaching study skills for dyslexic adults. Topics include: essay writing, exam revision, grammar, handwriting, memory, reading, spelling, time management and vocabulary building. *Contact information:* iANSYST Ltd, The White House, 72 Fen Road, Cambridge CB4 1UN. Tel: 01223 420101.

Lexia Institute – produces Lesson Planner for Windows and Macintosh so that all the essential resources for planning improved lessons quickly are at your fingertips. Lesson Planner includes:

- comprehensive sample plans to build on
- easy sharing of plans with colleagues
- instructional guidance
- extensive word lists with pronunciations
- Questions of the Day
- large print word lists for student use
- simple integration of plans

Contact information: Lexia Institute, 766 Raymundo Ave, Los Altos, CA 94024 Tel: (650) 964–3666; FAX: (650) 969–1632; email: Lexainst@aol.com/; Website: www.Lexianst.org

Numbershark is a program suitable for ages 6–adult and contains 30 games appropriate for a wide range of mathematical abilities. *Contact information:* iANSYST Ltd, The White House, 72 Fen Road, Cambridge CB4 1UN. Tel: 01223 420101.

Resources for Special Needs and Lower Achievers, the Thomas Nelson catalogue aimed at secondary schools, contains a comprehensive selection of programs to meet curriculum needs. *Contact information:* Tel: 01264 342992; email: schools@tips.co.uk; Website: www.nelson.co.uk

SuccessMaker is a computer-based integrated learning system designed to increase the level of basic skills in numeracy and literacy. It includes automatically individualised work programmes and teacher management tools and the materials are suitable for all ages from primary through to adult education. SuccessMaker is licensed to RM Learning Systems by Computer Curriculum, USA. For information regarding availability contact The Technology Colleges Trust. *Contact information:* Technology Colleges Trust, 9 Whitehall, London SW1A 2DD. Tel: 020 7839 9339; email: tctrust@rmplc.co.uk.

Xavier Software Educational Ltd supplies a wide range of programs designed to develop literacy skills. The programs are written in association with the Dyslexia Unit at Bangor University. *Contact information:* School of Psychology, University of Wales, Bangor, Gwynedd. Tel: 01248 382616; email: xavier@bangor.ac.uk; Website: http://xavier.bangor.ac.uk

Videos and books

The following sets of video tapes and accompanying books are all part of the Cap and Gown Series. Contact information is given after the details of the *A Level Mathematics* packages.

A Level Mathematics (agreed Common Core syllabus) is a very detailed course covering algebra, trigonometry, vectors, functions and all the fundamentals of the differential and integral calculus on seven video tapes running for over 20 hours. For further information contact: Cap and Gown Series. *Contact information:* for Cap and Gown Series of educational video tapes with books: Cap and Gown Series, PO Box 14, Penkridge, Stafford ST19 5SQ. Tel: 01785 713560.

English for 11–14s – Key Stage 3 is a set of two video tapes with a 50 page 'write-in' book.

Maths for 11–14s – Number and Algebra in Key Stage 3 is a set of three video tapes with a 980 page, 'write-in' book.

Mathematics in Key Stage 4 (Higher Tier) is a course for students expecting to achieve grades A, B or C and comprises six video tapes, two books and a question paper covering the complete two-year GCSE syllabus.

Mathematics in Key Stage 4 (Intermediate Tier) is a course for GCSE students expecting to achieve grades C, D or E and comprises four video tapes and two books covering all the number and algebra work in the two-year GCSE course.

Other materials

Cambridge Series   **Ruling 9**
These are exercise books that offer guidance to help improve handwriting available from Philip and Tacey. *Contact information:* Philip and Tacey, Northway, Andover, Hants. SP10 5BA. Tel: 01264 332171.

Fast Forward is a resource pack for developing study skills such as listening, organising, reading, note-taking, report writing and summarising. The material is in six separate topics each centred around a tape presentation. Each topic follows the same pattern and comprises a cassette tape, tape transcript (for teacher reference), pupil folder, extension work and answer sheets. Fast Forward is published by LDA (Dring, J. (1992) *Fast Forward.* Wisbech: LDA.). *Contact information:* LDA, Duke St, Wisbech, Cambs. PE13 2AE. Tel: 01945 463441.

The Handwriting File is suitable for ages 6–adult and contains a variety of exercises including timed handwriting exercises. *Contact information:* SEN Marketing, 18 Leeds Road, Outwood, Wakefield WF1 2LT. Tel/FAX: 01924 871697.

John Murray educational resources are a variety of materials available for use across the curriculum, including revision guides for individual GCSE and A Level subjects. *Contact information:* John Murray, 50 Albemarle Street, London W1S BD. Tel: 020 7493 4361.

Letts Revision Guides are available for GCSE and A Level courses. *Contact information:* Letts Educational, Freepost, Aldine Place, London W12 8BR. Tel: 0800 216592.

Lonsdale Revision Guides are available for GCSE courses. *Contact information:* Lonsdale Revision Guides, PO Box 7, Kirby Lonsdale, Lancashire LA6 2GD. Tel: 01524 272413.

Careers guidance

Centigrade is a questionnaire completed by students who intend to go on to further education. It is analysed by leading academic experts to provide a detailed career profile of courses which may appeal to students within the United Kingdom and the Republic of Ireland. For further information about this questionnaire, prices and other career advice contact Cambridge Occupational Analysts Ltd. *Contact information:* Cambridge Occupational Analysts Ltd, Sparham, Norwich NR98 5AQ. Tel: 01362 688722.

Degree Course Offers published in 1995 lists the AS/A Level or equivalent points required for single subject degree and HND courses in UK universities and colleges. It is published by Trotman and Co. Ltd, Surrey and is available from booksellers.

Financial Assistance for Students with Disabilites in Higher Education is published by and available from SKILL. *Contact information:* SKILL, Brixton Road, London SW9 7AA.

Higher Education and Disability is guide to higher education for people with disabilities. Published by Hobson Publishers and SKILL. *Contact information:* Hobson Publishers Ltd, 159–173 St Johns Street, London EC1B 4DR. Tel: 020 7335 6633.

The Perfect CV: How to get the job you really want (Jackson and Jackson 2000) offers advice on applying for jobs. It is published by Doubleday, London and is available from booksellers.

The Times Good University Guide 2001 is a useful source for information about UK universities. It is edited by John O'Leary *et al.* and published by Times Books in association with PWC, London and is available from booksellers.

UCAS Entrance Guide to HE in Scotland lists the entry requirements listed for degree and HND courses at all Scottish universities and HE Institutions. It is available from most booksellers.

UCAS website (http://www.ucas.ac.uk) gives instant access to university and college sites providing students with comprehensive information to all courses at UCAS institiutions.

University and College Entrance: The offical guide (The Big Guide) **(2001)** edited by T. Higgins is a strongly recommended reference book for degree courses and HND courses. It is published in Mansfield by Linney Group and is available from booksellers.

Useful addresses

The addresses and telephone numbers detailed here were correct at the time of publication.

Professional organisations and information centres

Advisory Centre for Education
1b Aberdeen Studios
22 Highbury Grove
London
N5 2EA
Tel: 020 7354 8321

Advisory Unit
126 Great North Road
Hatfield
Hertfordshire
AU1O 8AU
Tel: 01707 266714
Website: http://www:advisory-unit.org.uk

AUSTRALIA
SpELD NSW
129 Greenwich Road
Greenwich 2065
Sydney
NSW

Basic Skills Agency
7th Floor Commonwealth House
1/19 Oxford Street
London
WC1A 1NU
Tel: 020 7405 4017

BBC – UK on line education website
Information on foreign languages and GCSE and A Level revision help – www.bbc.education.co.uk

British Dyslexia Association (BDA)
98 London Road
Reading
RG1 5AU
Tel: 01189 662677
Website:
http://www.bda.demon.co.uk/;
email: Helpline: info@dyslexiahelp-bda.demon.co.uk

CANADA
Canadian Association for Children with Learning Difficulties
Maison Kildare House
323 Chapel Street
Suite 200
Ottawa
KIN 2Z2

Centre for Studies on Inclusive Education
1 Redland Close
Elm Lane
Redland
Bristol
BSE 6UE
Tel: 01179 238450

Children's Legal Centre
University of Essex
Wivenhoe Park
Colchester
Essex
CO4 3SQ
Tel: 01206 873820

Dyslexia, Dyspraxia and Attention Disorder Treatment Centre (DDAT)
6 The Square
Kenilworth
Warwickshire
CV8 1EB
Tel: 08450 250550; FAX: 01926 855727; Website: www.ddat.co.uk
email: infor@ddat.co.uk

Dyslexia Institute
133 Gresham Road
Staines
Middlesex
TW18 2AAJ
Tel: 01784 463851

Dyslexia Teaching Centre
23 Kensington Square
London W8
Tel: 020 7937 2408

Dyslexia Unit
University College of North Wales
Bangor
Gwynedd
LL57 2DG
Tel: 01248 351151 extension 2203 or 3841

European Dyslexia Association
Rue Defacquz 1
1000 Brussels
Tel: +32 2 537 0983; FAX: +32 2 537 9212; Website: http://www.eda-en.com; email: eda@kbnet.co.uk

Gifted Children's Information Centre (GCIC)
Director Dr Peter Condon
Hampton Grange
21 Hampton Lane
Solihull
B981 2QJ
Tel: 01217 054547
(Suppliers of books, guides, teaching packs and equipment for: gifted dyslexic and left-handed children. Psychological assessments, legal advice and guidance for children with special educational needs are also available.)

Helen Arkwell Dyslexia Centre
Frensham
Farnham
Surrey
GU10 3BW
Tel: 01252 792400

International Dyslexia Association
8600 La Salle Road
Chester Building
Suite 382
Baltimore
MD 21286-2044
USA
Tel: 001 410 296 0232;
FAX: 001 410 321 5069;
Website: http://www.interdys.org;
email: info@interdys.org

IPSEA (Independent Panel for Special Education)
22 Warren Hill Road
Woodbridge
Suffolk
1P12 4DU
Tel: 01394 380518

Lucid Creative Limited
PO Box 63
Beverley
East Yorkshire
HU 17 8ZZ
Tel/FAX: 01482 465589

Medway Dyslexia Centre
1 The Close
Rochester
ME1 1SD
Tel: 01634 848232

**National Association for Able
Children in Education (NACE)**
PO Box 242
Arnolds Way
Oxford
OX2 9FR
Tel: 01865 861879; FAX: 01865 861880

**National Association for Gifted
Children (NAGC)**
Elder House
Milton Keynes
MK9 1LR
Tel: 01908 673677

**National Association for Special
Educational Needs (NASEN)**
4–5 Amber Business Village
Amington
Tamworth
Staffs
B77 4RP
Tel: 01827 311500; FAX: 01827 313005;
email: welcome@nasen.org.uk

National Children's Bureau
8 Wakely Street
London
EC1V 7QE
Tel: 020 7843 6303

**National Council For Educational
Technology (NCET)**
Milburn Hill Road

Science Park
Coventry
CV4 7JJ
Tel: 01203 416994

National Listening Library
12 Lant Street
London
SE1 1QH
Tel: 020 7407 9417

National Literacy Association
Office No. 1
The Magistrates Court
Barngates
Christchurch
Dorset
BH23 1PY
Tel: 01202 484079/89; FAX: 01202
484079; email: nla@argonet.co.uk;
Website: www.nla.org.uk

Network 81
1 Woodfield Terrace
Chapel Hill
Stansted
Essex
CM24 8JA
Tel: 01279 647415

Scottish Dyslexia Association
Unit 3
Stirling Business Centre
Wellgreen
Stirling
FK8 2DZ
Tel: 01786 4466 650

The Arts Dyslexia Trust
Lodge Cottage
Brabourne Lees
Ashford
Kent
TN25 6QZ
Tel: 01303 813221

The Children's Society
Edward Rudolf House
Margery Street
London
WC1X 0JL

The Psychological Corporation
London Offices
24–28 Oval Road
London
NW1 7DX
Tel: 020 7424 4200; FAX: 020 7424
4457; email: TPC@TPC.HBUK.co.uk

The Royal College of Speech and Language Therapists
2 Whitehart Yard
London
SE1 1NX
Tel: 020 7378 1200

UNITED STATES
Association for Children with Learning Difficulties
5225 Grace Street
Pittsburgh
PA 152236

Learning Disabilities Association of America
4156 Library Road
Pittsburgh
Pennsylvania
15228
USA
Jean Patersen, National Executive
Director
Tel: 001 412 341 1515; FAX: 001 412
3344 0224

Orton Society
Chester Building
Suite 382
8600 La Salle Road
Baltimore
MD 21204

Examination boards

Edexcel
Stewart House
32 Russell Square
London
WC1B 5DN
Tel: 0870 240 9800
www.edexcel.org.uk

Midland Examining Group
Mill Warf
Mill Street
Birmingham
B6 4BU
Tel: 0121 628 2000

Northern Examination and Assessment Board
Devas Road
Manchester
M15 6EX
Tel: 0161 953 1180

Northern Ireland for curriculum Examinations and Assessment
Clarenden Road
Belfast
BT8 4RS
Tel: 028 9026 1200

OCR (Oxford, Cambridge and RSA Examinations)
Syndicate Buildings
1 Hills Road
Cambridge
CB1 2EU
Tel: 01223 552552

Oxford and Cambridge Schools Examination Board
(Oxford Office)
Elsfield Way
Oxford
OX2 8EP
Tel: 01865 552552

111

Scottish Examining Board
Ironmills Road
Dalkeith
Midlothian
EH22 1LE
Tel: 0131 663 6336

Southern Examining Group
Central Administration Office
Stag Hill House
Guildford
Surrey
GU2 5XJ
Tel: 01483 506506

Welsh Joint Education Committee
245 Western Avenue
Cardiff
CFS 2YX
Tel: 02920 265000

Suppliers of useful resources for secondary students with dyslexia

Ann Arbor
PO Box 1
Bedford
Northumberland
NE70 7JX
Tel: 01668 214460
FAX: 01668 214484

AVP
School Hill Centre
Chepstow
Monmouthshire
NP6 5PH
Tel: 01291 625439; FAX: 01291 629671; email: info@avp.co.uk

BECTa (British Educational Communication Technology Agency)
Millburn Hill Road
Science Park
Coventry
CV4 7U
Tel: 02476 416994; Website: http://becta.org.uk

Better Books
3 Paganel Drive
Dudley
West Midlands
DY 14AZ
Tel: 01384 253276

Cambridge University Press
Edinburgh Building
Shaftesbury Road
Cambs
CB2 2RU
Tel: 01223 312393

Collins Educational
Westerhill Rd
Bishopbriggs
Glasgow
G64 2QT
Tel: 0141 772 3200

Crick Software Ltd
1 The Avenue
Spinney Hill
Northampton
NN3 6BA
Tel: 01604 671691; FAX: 01604 671692; email: admin@cricksoft.com; Website: http://www.cricksoft.com/

David Fulton Publishers Ltd
The Chiswick Centre
414 Chiswick High Road
London
W4 5TF
Tel: 020 8996 3610; FAX: 020 8996 3622;
Website: http://www.
fultonpublishers.co.uk

Drake Educational
St Fagan's Rd
Fairwater
Cardiff
CF5 3AE

Dyslexia Unit
Dept of Psychology
University of Wales
Bangor
Gwynedd
LL57 2DG
Tel: 01248 382203

Gamz (Computer Software)
25 Albert Park Rd
Malvern
Worcs
WR14 1HW
Tel: 01684 562158

Ginn and Co Ltd
Linarce House
Gordon Hill
Oxford
OX2 HDP
Tel: 01865 888000

Heinemann Education
PO Box 380
Halley Court
Jordan Hill
Oxford
OX2 2QZ
Tel: 01865 314333

Hodder & Stoughton
Mill Rd
Dunton Green
Sevenoaks
Kent
TN13 2A
Tel: 01718 736000

Hornsby Resource Centre
Wye Street
London
SW11 2HB
Tel: 020 7223 1144

iANSYST Ltd (Computer Software)
The White House
72 Fen Rd
Cambridge
CB4 1UN
Tel: 01223 420101

IDL Centres Ltd
West Ancroft
Berwick-upon-Tweed
TD15 2DT
Tel: 01289 387076; Website:
http://www.idl-centres.co.uk

Inclusive Technology
Saddleworth Business Centre
Delph
Oldham
Ol3 5DF
Tel: 01457 819790; FAX: 01457
819799; email: inclusive@.co.uk

LDA (Learning Development Aids)
Duke Street
Wisbech
Cambs
PE13 2AE
Tel: 01945 463441

Learning Materials Ltd
Dixon Street
Wolverhampton
Tel: 01902 454026; FAX: 01902
457596; e-mail:
learning.materials@btinternet.com

MSL (Multi-sensory Learning) Ltd
32 Nene Valley Business Park
Oundle
Peterborough
PE8 4HL
Tel: 01823 289559

NFER-Nelson
Darville House
2 Oxford Rd East
Windsor
Berks
SL4 1DF
Tel: 01753 858961

Oxford University Press
Educational Supply Section
Saxon Way West
Corby
Northants
NN18 89BR
Tel: 01536 741519

Philip and Tacey
North Way
Andover
Hants
Tel: 01264 332171

**Read and Write Educational
Supplies**
Mount Pleasant
Mill Road
Aldington
Ashford
Kent
TN25 7AJ
Tel: 01233 720616

REM (Computer Software)
Great Western House
Langport
Somerset
TA10 9YU
Tel: 01458 253636

SEMERC
1 Broadbent Road
Watersheddings
Oldham
OL1 4LB
01616 274469

SEN Marketing
18 Leeds Rd
Outwood
Wakefield
WF1 2LT
Tel: 01924 871697

Special Needs Computing
Box 42
Rain Hill
Merseyside
L35 4RG
Tel: 01514 269988

Taskmaster Ltd
Morris Rd
Leicester
LE2 6BR
Tel: 01162 704286

Taylor & Francis Group
11 New Fetter Lane
London
EC4P 4EE
Tel: 020 7583 9855
Web site:
http://www.routledge.com/
routledge.html

Whurr Publishers Ltd
19b Compton Terrace
London
N1 2UN
Tel: 020 7359 5979; Website;
www.whurr.co.uk

Widgit Software
102 Radford Road
Leamington Spa
Warwicks
CV31 1LF
Tel: 01926 885303; Website:
http://www.widgit.com

Working abroad

Camp America
Tel: 020 7581 7333 (24-hour
telephone service)

Gap Activity Project (GAP)
Gap House
44 Queeen's Road
Reading
Berks
RG1 4BB
Tel: 01189 594914

Careers guidance

**Careers Services National
Association**
Ian Bourne
John's Cottage
Littleworth
Amberley
Stroud
GL5 5AL
Tel: 01453 872077; email:
exec@careers-uk.com; Website:
http://www.careers-uk.com

ISCO Careers Guidance
Regent's College
Regent's Park
London
Tel: 020 7487 3660

The Institute of Career Guidance
27a Lower High Street
Stourbridge
West Midlands
DY8 1TA
Library and Information Services –
Ellie Stevenson
Tel: 01384 445628/91/21; email:
ellie.stevenson@icg-uk.org
library@icg-uk.org; Website:
http://www.icg-uk.org

Bibliography

Acklaw, J. and Gupta, Y. (1989) 'Talking with parents of dyslexic children: the value of skilled discussion methods', in Hinson, M. (ed.) *Teachers and Special Educational Needs*, 198–203. London: Longman.

Armstrong, D. and Galloway, D. (1996) *Listening to Children in Education*. London: David Fulton Publishers.

Austen, J. (1972) *Pride and Prejudice*. Penguin English Library edition. London: Penguin Books.

Bennathan, M. (1988) 'Multiprofessional work', *Maladjustment and Therapeutic Education* **6**(2), 82–93.

Bullock, A. (1975) *A Language for Life*. London: HMSO.

Buzan, T (1991) *Use Your Head*. London: Open Books.

Carter, R. (1996) 'Dyslexia's broken bridge', *New Scientist* **119**, 142–57.

Chall, J. S. (1983) *Stages of Reading Development*. New York: McGraw-Hill.

Chall, J. S. *et al.* (1990) *The Reading Crisis: Why poor children fall behind*. Cambridge MA: Harvard University Press.

Christen, W. and Murphy, J. (1991) *Increasing Comprehension by Activating Prior Knowledge*. USA: ERIC Digest.

Clay, M. (1989) 'Observing young children reading texts', *Support for Learning* **4**(1) 7–9.

Cline, T. (1992) *The Assessment of Special Educational Needs: International perspectives*. London: Routledge.

Cook-Gumperz, J. (ed.) (1986) *The Social Construction of Literacy*. Cambridge: Cambridge University Press.

Daines, B. *et al.* (1996) *Spotlight on Special Educational Needs: Speech and language difficulties*. Stoke-on-Trent: Nasen Enterprises.

Davis, R. (1997) *The Gift of Dyslexia*. New York: Pedigree Books.

DeFries, J. (1991) 'Genetics and dyslexia', in Snowling, M. and Thomson, M. (eds) *Dyslexia: Integrating theory and practice*. London: Whurr Publishers.

Department of Education and Science (DES) (1981) *The Education Act*. London: HMSO.

DES (1970) *The Chronically Sick and Disabled Persons Act*. London: HMSO.

Dessent, T. (1987) *Making the Ordinary School Special*. Lewes: Falmer.

DFE (1994) *Code of Practice on the Identification and the Assessment of Special Educational Needs*. London: HMSO.

DfEE (1998) *The National Literacy Strategy: Framework for teaching.* London: HMSO.

DfEE (2001) *Special Educational Needs Code of Practice on the Identification and Assessment of Pupils with SEN,* Consultation document. London: HMSO.

DfES (2002) *Special Educational Needs Code of Practice 2001.* London: DfES (comes into effect January 2002).

Dring, J. (1992) *Fast Forward.* Wisbech: LDA.

Duane, D. (1991) 'Neurobiological issues in dyslexia', in Snowling, M. and Thomson, M. (eds) *Dyslexia: Integrating theory and practice.* London: Whurr Publishers.

Durlak, J. (1995) *Successful Prevention for Children and Adolescents.* London: Plenum Press.

Fenwick, E. and Smith, T. (1993) *Adolescence: The survival guide for parents and teenagers.* London: Dorling Kindersley.

Greenwold, L. (ed.) (2001) *Resources List.* Evesham: Patoss.

Gipps, C. and Stobart, G. (1993) *Assessment: A teacher's guide to the issues.* London: Hodder & Stoughton.

Gough, P. B. and Tunnmer, W. E. (1986) 'Decoding, reading, and reading disability', *Remedial and Special Education* **7**, 6–10.

Gregson, D. and Thewlis, S. (1983) *Comprehension and Research Skills.* Stafford: Nare Publications.

Harrison, C. and Coles, M. (eds) (1992) *The Reading for Real Handbook.* London: Routledge.

Hassett, J. (1984) *Psychology in Perspective.* New York: Harper Row.

Head, H. (1926) *Aphasia and Kindred Disorders of Speech.* London: Macmillan.

Hinshelwood, J. (1917) *Congenital Word Blindness.* London: K.H. Lewis.

Hinson, M. (ed.) (1989) *Teachers and Special Educational Needs.* London: Longman.

Hughes, R. (1989) 'A night in a cottage', in Sharrock, R. (ed.) *The Oxford Library of Classic Short Stories.* Oxford: Guild Publishing.

Hulme, C. and Snowling, M. (eds) (1994) *Reading Development and Dyslexia.* London: Whurr Publishers.

IDEA (1997) *Individuals with Disabilities Education Act.* Washington, USA: One Hundred Fifth Congress of the USA.

Ingram, J. and Worrall, N. (1993) *Teacher–Child Partnership: The negotiating classroom.* London: David Fulton Publishers.

Jacobs, V. A. (1999) 'What secondary teachers can do to teach reading: A three step strategy for helping students delve deeper into texts', *Harvard Education Letter* **15**, 4–5.

Jager Adams, M. (1990) 'Modelling the reading process', in Bilbey, N. (ed.) (1994) *Making Sense of Reading,* 40–60. Leamington Spa: Scholastic Publications.

Jones, N. (1990) 'Reader, writer, text', in Doughill, P. (ed.) *Developing English,* 155–67. London: Open University Press.

Jones, K. and Charlton, T. (1996) *Overcoming Learning and Behavioural Difficulties: Partnership with pupils*. London: Routledge.

Johnson, D. J. and Mykelebust, H. R. (1967) *Learning Disabilities, Education Principles and Practices*. New York: Grune and Stratton.

Kemp, P. (1997) *Integrated Learning Systems: A TC Trust project – first year report*. London: Technology Colleges Trust.

Kratoville, B. L. (1993) *Word Tracking: High frequency functional words*. USA: Ann Arbor Publishers.

Kussmaul, A. (1878) 'Word deafness and word blindness', in Von Ziemessen, H. (ed.) *Encyclopaedia of the Practice of Medicine*, Vol 14 (Diseases of the Nervous System and Disturbances of Speech). London: Maston, Searle and Rivington.

Lacey, P. and Lomas, J. (1993) *Support Services and the Curriculum*. London: David Fulton Publishers.

Lacey, P. and Ranson, S. (1994) 'Partnerships for learning', *Support for Learning* **9**, 79–82.

Levin, E. and Gibson, E. (1975) *The Psychology of Reading*. USA: Colonial Press.

MacBeath, J. *et al.* (2001) 'Switched on after hours', *Times Educational Supplement*, 15th June, 34.

Manford, P. (1991) 'Why collaborate?', *Special Children* **45**, 7–9.

McLean, B. (1993) 'Dyslexia style counsel', *Special Children* April, 9–11.

Meek, M. and Miller, J. (eds) (1992) *New Readings – Contribution to an Understanding of Literacy*. London: A & C Black Publishers.

Miles, E. (1991) 'Auditory dyslexia', in Snowling, M. and Thomson, M. (eds) *Dyslexia: Integrating theory and practice*, 187–95. London: Whurr Publishers.

Miles, T. (1983) *Dyslexia: The pattern of difficulties*. London: Routledge.

Miles, T. R. and Miles, E. (1990) *Dyslexia: A hundred years on*. Buckingham: Open University Press.

Moon, B. and Shelton Mayes, A. (1994) *Teaching and Learning in the Secondary School*. London: Routledge.

Moore, D. W. *et al.* (1999) 'Adolescent literacy: A position statement for the Commission on Adolescent Literacy of the International Reading Association', *Journal of Adolescent Literacy* **43**, 97–112.

Morgan, W. P. (1896) 'A case study of congenital word blindness', *British Medical Journal* **2**, 1378.

Nelson-Jones, R. (1986) *Human Relationship Skills*. London: Holt Rinehart.

NFER (1992) *Nelson Teachers' Guide*. Berkshire: NFER-Nelson.

Oakhill, J. V. and Garnham, A. (1988) *Becoming A Skilled Reader*. Oxford: Basil Blackwell.

Orton, S. (1937) *Reading Writing and Speech Problems in Children*. New York: W. W. Norton.

Paris, S. G. *et al.* (1983) 'Becoming a strategic reader', *Contemporary Educational Psychology* **8**, 293–316.

Paulesu, E. *et al.* (1996) 'Is developmental dyslexia a disconnection syndrome?' *Brain* **119**, 143–57.

Perfetti, C. A. (1985) *Reading Ability*. Oxford: Oxford University Press.

Perrone, V. (1994) 'How to engage students in learning', *Educational Leadership* **51**, 4–7.

Rogers, C. (1961) *On Becoming a Person*. Boston: Houghton Mifflin.

Russell, P. (1994) 'The Code of Practice: new partnerships for children with special educational needs', *British Journal of Education* **21**(2), 48–52.

Smith, R. (1992) 'I blame the parents...', *Child Education* August, 42–3.

Stanovich, K. E. *et al.* (1988) 'The developmental lag hypothesis in reading: Longitudinal and matched reading-level comparisons', *Child Development* **59**, 71–86.

Stanovich, K. E. (1991) 'The theoretical and practical consequences of discrepancy definitions of dyslexia', in Snowling, M. and Thomson, M. (eds) *Dyslexia: Integrating theory and practice*. London: Whurr Publishers.

Stein, J. F. (1991) 'Vision and language' in Snowling, M. and Thomson, M. (eds) *Dyslexia: Integrating theory and practice*. London: Whurr Publishers.

Steinbeck, J. (1937) *Of Mice and Mice*. London: Heinemann.

Stirling, E. G. (1985) *Help for the Dyslexic Adolescent*. Bristol: St. Davids's College.

Stobart, G. and Gipps, C. (1990) *Assessment: A teacher's guide to the issues*. London: Hodder and Stoughton Educational.

Stordy, J. (1997) 'Dyslexia, attention deficit hyperactivity disorder, dyspraxia – do fatty acids help?', *Dyslexia Review* **98**(2), 1–3.

Stothard, S. E. (1994) 'The Nature and treatment of reading comprehension difficulties in children', in Hulme, L. and Snowling, M. (eds) *Reading Development and Dyslexia*, 200–31. London: Whurr Publishers.

Thomas, G. (1991) *Effective Classroom Teamwork: Support or intrusion?* London: Routledge.

Thomas, D. (1991) 'A framework for teaching reading', *Support for Learning* **6**(3), 103–07.

Tizard, J. (1972) *Children with Specific Reading Difficulties*. London: HMSO.

Townsend, S. (1982) *The Secret Diary of Adrian Mole Aged 13³/₄*. London: Methuen.

Traves, P. (1992) 'Reading: the entitlement to be "properly literate"' in Meek, M. and Millar, J. (eds) *New Readings – Contribution to an Understanding of Literacy*, 17–25. London: A. & C. Black Publications.

Turner, M. (1991) 'Finding out: the reading debate', *Support for Learning* **6**(3), 99–101.

Vacca, R. T. (1998) 'Let's not marginalize adolescent literacy' *Journal of Adolescent and Adult Literacy* **41**, 604–9.

Vellutino, F. R. (1987) 'Dyslexia' *Scientific American* **256**(3), 20–7.

Warnock, M. (1978) *Special Educational Needs*. (Report of the Committee of Enquiry into the Special Education of Handicapped Children and Young People). London: HMSO.

West, T. (1997) *In the Mind's Eye*. New York: Prometheus Books.

Westall, R. (1975) *The Machine Gunners*. London: Macmillan Publishers.

Wiske, M. S. (ed.) (1998) *Teaching for Understanding: Linking research with practice*. San Francisco, CA: Jossey-Bass.

Zangwill, O. L. and Blakemore, C. B. (1972) 'Dyslexia – a reversal of eye movements during reading', *Neuropsychologia* **10**, 371–5.